T0128015

CONFESSING *and* PRAYING
the
WORD OF GOD

"And Jesus said unto them, I am the bread of life: he that cometh to me
shall never hunger; and he that believeth on me shall never thirst."
—John 6:35

Vickie Prince

WESTBOW
PRESS®
A DIVISION OF THOMAS NELSON
& ZONDERVAN

WestBow Press books may be ordered through booksellers or by contacting:

WestBow Press
A Division of Thomas Nelson & Zondervan
1663 Liberty Drive
Bloomington, IN 47403
www.westbowpress.com
1 (866) 928-1240

ISBN: 978-1-5127-5393-6 (sc)
ISBN: 978-1-5127-5394-3 (hc)
ISBN: 978-1-5127-5392-9 (e)

Library of Congress Control Number: 2016913897

Print information available on the last page.

WestBow Press rev. date: 01/09/2019

Presented to

_____

By

_____

Date

_____

Occasion

_____

"For all the promises of God in him are yea, and
in him Amen, unto the glory of God by us."
—*2 Corinthians 1:20*

Dedication

This book is dedicated first to my Father God, who inspired me to write this book for his family, the body of his Son, Jesus Christ. Thank you, Father, for placing in me a zeal and a passion to reach the masses for you in a way that would lead them to a closer relationship with you. Thank you for not letting me give up on fulfilling your plan and destiny for my life. Thank you for being so specific concerning every detail of this book, from the front to the back cover. You truly are an awesome God, and I love you so much!

I dedicate this book to my husband, Elder Ollie D'Wayne Prince, who has been such a rock for me. He has been such an encouragement to me to finish the work God has started in me. His love, strength, and support for me have been so amazing in the development of this book. I am so thankful to God that I have been able to draw from and lean on his spiritual wisdom and knowledge of God's word. He has also spent countless hours in prayer with me and for me, that God's perfect and complete will for this book would be done. I love you, husband!

I also dedicate this book to my daughters Victoria, Adriana, and Jarielle, who are the original recipients of these confessional scriptures when they were very young. They have now matured into such beautiful young women that their father and I are so proud of. Thank you, girls, for pouring your insight and wisdom into the formation of this book.

Contents

Special Prayers

Words from God Almighty

"Therefore shall ye lay up these my words in your heart and in your soul, and bind them for a sign upon your hand, that they may be as frontlets between your eyes.

And ye shall teach them your children, speaking of them when thou sittest in thine house, and when thou walkest by the way, when thou liest down, and when thou risest up.

And thou shalt write them upon the door posts of thine house, and upon thy gates:

That your days may be multiplied, and the days of your children; in the land which the LORD sware unto your fathers to give them, as the days of heaven upon the earth."

—Deuteronomy 11:18–21

Introduction

This book was inspired by my desire to have a daily personal meditation and confession of the word of God in a way that was deeper than what I was experiencing. It was birthed in my spirit at a time when I needed a more intimate relationship with God and for him to answer some needed prayers in my life. God inspired me to start writing these scriptures over twenty-five years ago for our family, friends, and various churches we would minister to. But recently, Father God instructed me to prepare these scriptures to impact the whole body of Christ.

Many countless hours, days, and nights have been spent before God, receiving his explicit instructions on different subjects and specific scriptures to use for this book. So I can say with a holy conviction that you are about to receive the very heart, purpose, and plan of God that will impact the rest of your life.

I believe that this book will not only inspire your faith and cause you to grow spiritually, but it will also activate spiritual truths in your life. Confessions and faith in the word of God will allow you to see manifestations of different levels of your prayer life unfold before you.

This book will cause your faith to grow to a level that will bring what you are confessing and believing God for from the realm of the spirit into the natural realm. So I urge you to not allow this book to become a shelf book but to keep it handy and touch it daily so you will experience an awesome time of fellowship with your Father daily. This book is not a seasonal book that you visit and read once or use for one specific issue in your life. This book should be used continually to confess and pray scriptures to God on a daily basis for your whole life.

I believe that the confession of scriptures, speaking God's word to him from our hearts, is something that every believer desires to do but hasn't really known how to do. This book will help you with that. From the start of this book to the end, you will experience such a hunger and thirst for more of God and his word. For the Bible teaches, "Man shall not live by bread alone, but by every word that proceeds out of the mouth of God" *(Matthew 4:4)*.

It is so vitally important that we make positive confessions over our lives and over the lives of the ones we love by speaking the word of God from our hearts, for the Bible says in Psalm 103:20, "Bless the Lord, ye his angels, that excel in strength, that do his commandments, hearkening unto the voice of his word." So when we speak God's word, he hears it, his angels hear it, and they do what the word of the Lord says. It's the same when we speak negative words; the enemy also hears them and goes about activating those words as well.

With the leading of the Holy Spirit, I have personalized these scriptures in a way that will help lead you directly into the presence of God. The wording of the scriptures in this book will allow you to worship and speak to God, speak to our Lord Jesus Christ, and speak to the Holy Spirit in such an intimate and personal way. You will not only find it easy to confess God's word on a daily basis; you will also find it enjoyable. These scriptures will not only strengthen you but also cause you to grow in the knowledge of what the word of God says concerning many situations in your life.

These confessional scriptures have been vital to my family for many years. We began monitoring the words of our children at their early ages because we knew that the words that would come out of their mouths would also shape their worlds. So in our home, we were quick to correct any negative spoken words. These scriptures have caused tremendous growth and increase in our lives since then, for the Bible says, "So then faith cometh by hearing, and hearing by the word of God" *(Romans 10:17).*

By confessing God's word continually, daily, you will be changed in your mind, changed in your body, and changed in your spirit. You will also experience change in your home and in your environment. You will begin to experience the presence of God at a whole new level. Mostly, you will express your heart to God, but he will also express his heart to you. God so desires to hear his children's voices daily.

One day you may have a need for peace and the next day you may have a need for joy, but whenever you begin to confess the word of God, always start with praise and adoration. It is our way of speaking to God first before asking him for something. How would we like it if our children came to us asking for things before saying, "Hi, Mom or Dad, how are you today?" It's the same way with God. He wants our reverence first, and then we can pray those other things to him.

Can you visualize what would happen when a congregation begins to pray the scriptures in "Prayer for the Church" in one accord? This will allow a local church to pray corporately the bountiful blessings of God over a church body. And we, as a church body, get to confess the unity that God so desires that we walk in, so that he can release his glory as we enter into his presence.

Also in "Prayer for Pastors" is where we, a church body, get to pray an ample supply of scriptures over the leaders of the flocks of God. We often desire to pray for our pastors but find we have limited thoughts and words of what to pray. In this section, your words will not run dry until you have completely saturated your pastors with the word of God and with prayer.

You will find confessing these scriptures to be so addictive and powerful, with one scripture continually leading to the next scripture.

So don't just read these words but verbally speak them from your heart to God, and you will experience such a close connection with him that will fill you with an abundance of the fruit of his Spirit. I pray your heart and soul become so flooded with immense peace and joy that lead you directly into the presence of Almighty God and that you will experience such a personal and intimate relationship with him that you have never known. He is waiting to hear from you!

~ 1 ~

Praise and Adoration

I love you, Father, and I live to worship and praise you gloriously. You are my life, and your breath is the very air that I breathe.

With my voice, with all my heart and with all my strength, I give you praise. I sing a new song to you with my spirit, O Lord, and I praise and worship you in spirit and in truth.

My heart longs to commune with you and to become more intimate with you, so that I may know your heart and understand your ways. My soul pants for you, O God, and my soul thirsts for you, O Living God.

Right now, I give you all of me. I give you all the praise and all the glory for all that you are and for who you are to me. Thank you, Father, that

This is the day which you have made,
O Lord; I rejoice and I am glad in it.
—Psalm 118:24

I bless you, O Lord, at all times: your praise
is continually in my mouth.
—Psalm 34:1

My voice you hear in the morning, O Lord; in the
morning I direct my prayer unto you, and I look up.
—Psalm 5:3

I sing unto you, O Lord, I bless your name; I
show forth your salvation from day to day.
—*Psalm 96:2*

I declare your glory among the heathen,
your wonders among all people.
—*Psalm 96:3*

I come and worship before you, O Lord; and I glorify your name.
—*Psalm 86:9*

For you, O Lord, are high above all the earth:
you are exalted far above all gods.
—*Psalm 97:9*

I praise your name, O Lord: for your name alone is
excellent; your glory is above the earth and heaven.
—*Psalm 148:13*

Honour and majesty are before you: strength
and beauty are in your sanctuary.
—*Psalm 96:6*

I make a joyful noise unto you, O Lord.
—*Psalm 100:1*

I serve you with gladness: I come before
your presence with singing.
—*Psalm 100:2*

I enter into your gates with thanksgiving, and into your courts
with praise: I am thankful unto you, and I bless your name.
—*Psalm 100:4*

For you are good, O Lord; your mercy is everlasting;
and your truth endures to all generations.
—*Psalm 100:5*

I give unto you, O Lord, the glory due unto your
name; I worship you, in the beauty of holiness.
—*Psalm 29:2*

I lift up my hands in the sanctuary, and I bless you, O Lord.
—*Psalm 134:2*

O God, you are my God; early I seek you: my soul thirsts for you,
my flesh longs for you in a dry and thirsty land, where no water is.
—*Psalm 63:1*

I long to see your power and your glory, O God,
so as I have seen you in the sanctuary.
—*Psalm 63:2*

Because your lovingkindness is better than life,
my lips praise you.
—*Psalm 63:3*

Thus I bless you while I live: I lift up my hands in your name.
—*Psalm 63:4*

My soul is satisfied as with marrow and fatness;
and my mouth praise you with joyful lips.
—*Psalm 63:5*

I remember you, O Lord, upon my bed, and I
meditate on you in the night watches.
—*Psalm 63:6*

Because you are my help, therefore in the
shadow of your wings I rejoice.
—*Psalm 63:7*

My soul follows hard after you, O Lord:
your right hand upholds me.
—*Psalm 63:8*

Glory and honour are in your presence; strength
and gladness are in your place.
—*1 Chronicles 16:27*

As the hart pants after the water brooks, so
pants my soul after you, O God.
—*Psalm 42:1*

Bless the Lord, O my soul: and all that is within
me, Lord, I bless your holy name.
—*Psalm 103:1*

My tongue speaks of your righteousness
and of your praise all the day long.
—*Psalm 35:28*

You have formed me for yourself, O Lord; I show forth your praise.
—*Isaiah 43:21*

By Jesus therefore I offer the sacrifice of praise to you, O God,
continually, that is, the fruit of my lips giving thanks to your name.
—*Hebrews 13:15*

I let my mouth be filled with your praise
and with your honour all the day.
—*Psalm 71:8*

I speak to myself in psalms and hymns and spiritual songs,
singing and making melody in my heart to you, O Lord.
—*Ephesians 5:19*

I give thanks always for all things unto you, O God
my Father, in the name of my Lord Jesus Christ.
—*Ephesians 5:20*

And now my head is lifted up above my enemies round
about me: therefore I offer in your tabernacle sacrifices
of joy; I sing, yea, I sing praises unto you, O Lord.
—*Psalm 27:6*

~ 2 ~

God's Kingdom and Glory

Father God, I thank you that your kingdom is not of this world but it is a heavenly kingdom where you reign as Lord and King over all.

Your word declares that your kingdom is an everlasting kingdom and that it has no end. You desire that I daily live a kingdom lifestyle and partake of all the wealth and all the provisions that you have provided for me in your kingdom.

I understand that I am a citizen of your kingdom, O God, and that I have citizen rights and privileges that allow me to live and walk in all of your fullness and all the benefits of your kingdom. Therefore,

> I seek first your kingdom, O God, and your righteousness;
> and all these things are added unto me.
> —*Matthew 6:33*

> O Lord, you have prepared your throne in the
> heavens; and your kingdom rules over all.
> —*Psalm 103:19*

> You, O God, are the King of all the earth: I
> sing praises with understanding.
> —*Psalm 47:7*

> O God, you reign over the heathen: God, you
> sit upon the throne of your holiness.
> —*Psalm 47:8*

Wherefore I receive a kingdom which cannot be
moved, I have grace, whereby I serve you, O God,
acceptably with reverence and godly fear.
—*Hebrews 12:28*

For the kingdom is yours, O Lord: and you
are the governor among the nations.
—*Psalm 22:28*

Father, your city has no need of the sun, neither
of the moon, to shine in it: for your glory, O God,
lightens it, and the Lamb is the light thereof.
—*Revelation 21:23*

The heavens declare your glory, O God; and
the firmament shows your handywork.
—*Psalm 19:1*

O Lord, the tabernacle is sanctified by your glory.
—*Exodus 29:43*

With open face, I behold as in a glass your glory,
O Lord, I am changed into the same image from
glory to glory, even as by your Spirit, O Lord.
—*2 Corinthians 3:18*

For I reckon that the sufferings of this present time are not worthy
to be compared with the glory which shall be revealed in me.
—*Romans 8:18*

Yours, O Lord, is the greatness, and the power, and the
glory, and the victory, and the majesty: for all that is
in heaven and in earth is yours; yours is the kingdom,
O Lord, and you are exalted as head above all.
—*1 Chronicles 29:11*

Both riches and honour come of you, O Lord, and you reign
over all; and in your hand is power and might; and in your
hand it is to make great, and to give strength unto all.
—1 Chronicles 29:12

O God, how great are your signs! and how mighty are
your wonders! Your kingdom is an everlasting kingdom,
and your dominion is from generation to generation.
—Daniel 4:3

Your kingdom, O God, comes not with observation.
—Luke 17:20

Neither shall I say, Lo here! or, lo there! for, behold,
your kingdom, O God, is within me.
—Luke 17:21

For you, O God, are a consuming fire.
—Hebrews 12:29

By you, Lord Jesus, I have access by faith into this grace
wherein I stand, and I rejoice in hope of your glory, O God.
—Romans 5:2

Lord, I speak of the glory of your kingdom,
and I talk of your power.
—Psalm 145:11

I make known to the sons of men your mighty acts, and
the glorious majesty of your kingdom, O Lord.
—Psalm 145:12

Your kingdom is an everlasting kingdom, and your
dominion endures throughout all generations.
—Psalm 145:13

Your kingdom come, O Lord. Your will be
done in earth, as it is in heaven.
—*Matthew 6:10*

Father, you have delivered me from the power of darkness,
and have translated me into the kingdom of your dear Son.
—*Colossians 1:13*

Your kingdom, O God, is not in word, but in power.
—*1 Corinthians 4:20*

For so an entrance is ministered unto me abundantly into the
everlasting kingdom of my Lord and Saviour Jesus Christ.
—*2 Peter 1:11*

I am born of water and of the Spirit, I enter
into your kingdom, O God.
—*John 3:5*

I am unto you, O Lord, a kingdom of priests, and an holy nation.
—*Exodus 19:6*

For your kingdom, O God, is not meat and drink; but
righteousness, and peace, and joy in the Holy Ghost.
—*Romans 14:17*

Your throne, O God, is for ever and ever: the
sceptre of your kingdom is a right sceptre.
—*Psalm 45:6*

~ 3 ~

Jesus Christ

I worship you, Lord Jesus Christ, because you are the Second Person of the Godhead Trinity and I confess you are my Lord.

Thank you, my Savior, for loving me so much that you would leave your holy throne and sacrifice your life for me by dying for my sins. Because of your sacrifice, I have eternal life.

You purchased my salvation with your scars, you suffered in my place, you died on the cross, and you rose from the grave to pay for my sins. Thank you, Lord Jesus, for bridging the gap and removing the veil that was between my Father and me.

Thank you, Lord Jesus, for always leading me to my Father, so that I can commune with him and bring him honor and glory. Therefore,

I look unto you, Lord Jesus, the author and finisher
of my faith; who for the joy that was set before you
endured the cross, despising the shame, and you are
set down at the right hand of the throne of God.
—*Hebrews 12:2*

I consider you, Lord Jesus, that endured such contradiction of
sinners against yourself, lest I be wearied and faint in my mind.
—*Hebrews 12:3*

Lord Jesus, you are the way, the truth, and the life:
I come not unto the Father, but by you.
—*John 14:6*

Jesus Christ, you are the same yesterday, and to day, and for ever.
—*Hebrews 13:8*

For other foundation can no man lay than that
is laid, which is you, Jesus Christ.
—*1 Corinthians 3:11*

Lord Jesus, your kingdom is not of this world.
—*John 18:36*

Now I am clean through the word which
you have spoken unto me, O Lord.
—*John 15:3*

For there is one God, and one mediator between
God and men, the man Christ Jesus.
—*1 Timothy 2:5*

Blessed are you, O God and Father of my Lord Jesus Christ, which
according to your abundant mercy have begotten me again unto
a lively hope by the resurrection of Jesus Christ from the dead.
—*1 Peter 1:3*

Lord Jesus, you are the good shepherd:
you give your life for the sheep.
—*John 10:11*

Lord Jesus, you are the image of the invisible
God, the firstborn of every creature.
—*Colossians 1:15*

For by you were all things created, that are in heaven,
and that are in earth, visible and invisible, whether they
be thrones, or dominions, or principalities, or powers:
all things were created by you, and for you, O Lord.
—*Colossians 1:16*

And you are before all things, Lord Jesus,
and by you all things consist.
—*Colossians 1:17*

Lord Jesus, you are the head of the body, the church:
you are the beginning, the firstborn from the dead; that
in all things you might have the preeminence.
—*Colossians 1:18*

For it pleased the Father that in you, Lord
Jesus, should all fullness dwell.
—*Colossians 1:19*

And, having made peace through the blood of your cross, Lord
Jesus, by you to reconcile all things unto yourself; by you, I
say, whether they be things in earth, or things in heaven.
—*Colossians 1:20*

By you, Lord Jesus, I have access by faith into this grace
wherein I stand, and I rejoice in hope of your glory, O God.
—*Romans 5:2*

Lord Jesus, you being the brightness of your glory, and the
express image of your person, and upholding all things by the
word of your power, when you had by yourself purged my
sins, sat down on the right hand of the Majesty on high.
—*Hebrews 1:3*

Many other signs truly you did, Lord Jesus, in the presence
of your disciples, which are not written in this book.
—*John 20:30*

But these are written, that I might believe that you,
Lord Jesus, are the Christ, the Son of God; and that
believing I might have life through your name.
—*John 20:31*

I joy in you, O God, through my Lord Jesus Christ,
by whom I have now received the atonement.
—Romans 5:11

Lord Jesus, you are the Word and you were made flesh, and
dwelt among us, and we beheld your glory, the glory as of
the only begotten of the Father, full of grace and truth.
—John 1:14

For the law was given by Moses, but grace
and truth came by you, Jesus Christ.
—John 1:17

I am sanctified through the offering of your
body, Jesus Christ, once for all.
—Hebrews 10:10

O God, you are faithful, by you I was called unto the
fellowship of your Son Jesus Christ my Lord.
—1 Corinthians 1:9

For I determined not to know any thing among
others, save Jesus Christ, and him crucified.
—1 Corinthians 2:2

My conversation is in heaven; from whence also I
look for my Saviour, my Lord Jesus Christ.
—Philippians 3:20

My tongue confess that Jesus Christ is Lord,
to the glory of God my Father.
—Philippians 2:11

For my Maker is my husband; the Lord of hosts is
your name; and my Redeemer the Holy One of Israel;
The God of the whole earth you are called.
—*Isaiah 54:5*

Lord Jesus, you are the Christ, the Son of the living God.
—*Matthew 16:16*

For though I have ten thousand instructors in Christ,
yet have I not many fathers: for in you, Christ
Jesus, I am begotten though the gospel.
—*1 Corinthians 4:15*

For so an entrance is ministered unto me abundantly into the
everlasting kingdom of my Lord and Saviour Jesus Christ.
—*2 Peter 1:11*

For I know the grace of my Lord Jesus Christ, that,
though you were rich, yet for my sake you became
poor, that I through your poverty might be rich.
—*2 Corinthians 8:9*

In you, Lord Jesus, are hid all the treasures
of wisdom and knowledge.
—*Colossians 2:3*

Lord Jesus, you have obtained a more excellent ministry,
by how much also you are the mediator of a better
covenant, which was established upon better promises.
—*Hebrews 8:6*

But you, Jesus Christ, being come an high priest of good
things to come, by a greater and more perfect tabernacle,
not made with hands, that is to say, not of this building;
—*Hebrews 9:11*

Neither by the blood of goats and calves, but by your
own blood you entered in once into the holy place,
having obtained eternal redemption for me.
—*Hebrews 9:12*

For if the blood of bulls and of goats, and the ashes of an heifer
sprinkling the unclean, sanctifies to the purifying of the flesh:
—*Hebrews 9:13*

How much more shall your blood, Jesus Christ, who through
the eternal Spirit offered yourself without spot to God, purge
my conscience from dead works to serve the living God?
—*Hebrews 9:14*

And for this cause you, Lord Jesus, are the mediator of the new
testament, that by means of death, for the redemption of the
transgressions that were under the first testament, they which
are called might receive the promise of eternal inheritance.
—*Hebrews 9:15*

Whom having not seen, I love; in whom, though
now I see you not, Lord Jesus, yet believing, I
rejoice with joy unspeakable and full of glory.
—*1 Peter 1:8*

Seeing then that I have a great high priest, that is passed into
the heavens, Jesus the Son of God, I hold fast my profession.
—*Hebrews 4:14*

Christ, as a son over your own house; whose house am I, I hold fast
the confidence and the rejoicing of the hope firm unto the end.
—*Hebrews 3:6*

I am made a partaker of you, Jesus Christ, I hold the
beginning of my confidence steadfast unto the end.
—*Hebrews 3:14*

For if by one man's offence death reigned by one; much
more I which receive abundance of grace and of the gift of
righteousness shall reign in life by one, Jesus Christ.
—*Romans 5:17*

But I see you, Lord Jesus, you were made a little lower than
the angels for the suffering of death, crowned with glory and
honour; that you by the grace of God should taste death for me.
—*Hebrews 2:9*

For it became you, Lord Jesus, for whom are all things, and
by whom are all things, in bringing me unto glory, to make
the captain of my salvation perfect through sufferings.
—*Hebrews 2:10*

The name of my Lord Jesus Christ is glorified in me, and I in him,
according to the grace of my God and my Lord Jesus Christ.
—*2 Thessalonians 1:12*

For you, Jesus Christ, also have once suffered for sins, the
just for the unjust, that you might bring me to God, being
put to death in the flesh, but quickened by the Spirit.
—*1 Peter 3:18*

I am a partaker of your heavenly calling, O God, I consider
the Apostle and High Priest of my profession, Christ Jesus.
—*Hebrews 3:1*

I believe on you, Lord Jesus, I have everlasting life.
—*John 6:47*

Lord Jesus, you are that bread of life.
—*John 6:48*

Lord Jesus, you are the bread which comes down
from heaven, that I eat thereof, and not die.
—*John 6:50*

Lord Jesus, you are the living bread which came down from
heaven: I eat of this bread, I live for ever: and the bread
that you give is your flesh, which you give for my life.
—*John 6:51*

I have such an high priest, who is set on the right hand
of the throne of the Majesty in the heavens.
—*Hebrews 8:1*

Lord Jesus, you are a priest for ever after the order of Melchisedec.
—*Hebrews 7:17*

But now in you, Christ Jesus, I who sometimes
was far off am made nigh by your blood.
—*Ephesians 2:13*

I believe on you, Lord Jesus Christ, and I am saved, and my house.
—*Acts 16:31*

I have therefore, boldness to enter into the
holiest by your blood, Lord Jesus.
—*Hebrews 10:19*

In you I have redemption through your blood, Lord Jesus, the
forgiveness of sins, according to the riches of your grace.
—*Ephesians 1:7*

The grace of my Lord Jesus Christ, and your love, O God,
and the communion of the Holy Ghost, is with me. Amen.
—2 Corinthians 13:14

Lord Jesus, you are He that lives, and was dead;
and, behold, you are alive for evermore, Amen;
and have the keys of hell and of death.
—Revelation 1:18

I hear your word, Lord Jesus, and I believe on him that
sent you, I have everlasting life, and I shall not come into
condemnation; but I am passed from death unto life.
—John 5:24

Jesus Christ, you are the faithful witness, and the first begotten
of the dead, and the prince of the kings of the earth. Unto you
that loved me, and washed me from my sins in your own blood,
—Revelation 1:5

And you, Lord Jesus, have made me a king and
priest unto God and your Father; to him be glory
and dominion for ever and ever. Amen.
—Revelation 1:6

Behold, Lord Jesus, you come with clouds; and every eye shall
see you, and they also which pierced you: and all kindreds
of the earth shall wail because of you. Even so, Amen.
—Revelation 1:7

You are Alpha and Omega, the beginning and the ending, O Lord,
which is, and which was, and which is to come, the Almighty.
—Revelation 1:8

Lord Jesus, you are Alpha and Omega, the first and the last.
—Revelation 1:11

~ 4 ~

The Holy Spirit

I thank you, Holy Spirit, for dwelling in me and for speaking to my spirit the heart of God. Holy Spirit, you bear witness with my spirit that I am God's child.

You are faithful to lead and guide me into all areas of truth, and I thank you for always leading me to my Lord and Savior, Jesus Christ. Thank you for constantly communing with my spirit the word of God and the will of God, that I may be complete in him.

Because my body is your temple, Holy Spirit, I choose to walk in holiness, in complete submission to your leading, and I choose not to grieve you with sin. Therefore,

I live in the Spirit, I also walk in the Spirit.
—*Galatians 5:25*

My body is the temple of the Holy Ghost which is in
me, which I have of God, and I am not my own.
—*1 Corinthians 6:19*

I grieve not the holy Spirit of God, whereby I
am sealed unto the day of redemption.
—*Ephesians 4:30*

A new heart also you have given me, O Lord, and a new spirit
you have put within me: and you have taken away the stony
heart out of my flesh, and you have given me a heart of flesh.
—*Ezekiel 36:26*

O Lord, you put your spirit within me, and cause me to walk
in your statutes, and I keep your judgments, and I do them.
—Ezekiel 36:27

Your spirit, O Lord, rests upon me, the spirit of wisdom
and understanding, the spirit of counsel and might, the
spirit of knowledge and of the fear of the Lord.
—Isaiah 11:2

I am filled with the Holy Ghost, and I speak with
other tongues, as the Spirit gives me utterance.
—Acts 2:4

I am not in the flesh, but in the Spirit, for
the Spirit of God dwells in me.
—Romans 8:9

The Spirit also helps my infirmities: for I know not what
I should pray for as I ought: but the Spirit itself makes
intercession for me with groanings which cannot be uttered.
—Romans 8:26

In you, Lord Jesus, I also trusted, after that I heard the word
of truth, the gospel of my salvation: in whom also after that
I believed, I was sealed with that holy Spirit of promise.
—Ephesians 1:13

The Spirit itself bears witness with my
spirit, that I am your child, O God.
—Romans 8:16

I build up myself on my most holy faith, praying in the Holy Ghost.
—Jude 1:20

But the Comforter, which is the Holy Ghost, whom the Father has sent in your name, Lord Jesus, he teaches me all things, and brings all things to my remembrance, whatsoever you have said unto me.
—*John 14:26*

Your Spirit, O God, that raised up Jesus from the dead dwells in me, you that raised up Christ from the dead also quickens my mortal body by your Spirit that dwells in me.
—*Romans 8:11*

Lord God, you are a Spirit: and I worship you in spirit and in truth.
—*John 4:24*

Now you, O Lord, are that Spirit: and where your Spirit is, there is liberty.
—*2 Corinthians 3:17*

I am led by your Spirit, O God, I am your son, O God.
—*Romans 8:14*

I quench not the Spirit.
—*1 Thessalonians 5:19*

I am the temple of God, and your Spirit, O God, dwells in me.
—*1 Corinthians 3:16*

In you, Lord Jesus, I also am built together for an habitation of God through the Spirit.
—*Ephesians 2:22*

Hope makes me not ashamed; because your love, O God, is shed abroad in my heart by the Holy Ghost which is given unto me.
—*Romans 5:5*

Holy Spirit, you are the Spirit of truth; whom the world
cannot receive, because it sees you not, neither knows you:
but I know you; for you dwell with me, and you are in me.
—John 14:17

The anointing which I have received of you, Lord Jesus,
abides in me, and I need not that any man teaches me: but
as the same anointing teaches me of all things, and is truth,
and is no lie, and even as it has taught me, I abide in him.
—1 John 2:27

I am not drunk with wine, wherein is excess;
but I am filled with the Spirit.
—Ephesians 5:18

I am baptized with the Holy Ghost, and with fire.
—Matthew 3:11

I believe on you, Lord Jesus, as the scripture has said,
out of my belly flow rivers of living water.
—John 7:38

I walk in the Spirit, and I do not fulfil the lust of the flesh.
—Galatians 5:16

Holy Ghost, you teach me in the same hour what I ought to say.
—Luke 12:12

My eye has not seen, nor my ear heard, neither have
entered into my heart, the things which you, O God,
have prepared for me because I love you.
—1 Corinthians 2:9

But you, O God, have revealed them unto me by your Spirit:
for the Spirit searches all things, yea, the deep things of God.
—1 Corinthians 2:10

Now I have received, not the spirit of the world, but
the spirit which is of God; that I might know the
things that are freely given to me of you, O God.
—*1 Corinthians 2:12*

Which things also I speak, not in the words which
man's wisdom teaches, but which the Holy Ghost
teaches; comparing spiritual things with spiritual.
—*1 Corinthians 2:13*

Heavenly Father, you give the Holy Spirit to me because I ask you.
—*Luke 11:13*

I repent, and I am baptized in the name of Jesus Christ for the
remission of sins, and I receive the gift of the Holy Ghost.
—*Act 2:38*

It is the spirit that quickens; the flesh profits nothing: the words that
you speak unto me, Lord Jesus, they are spirit, and they are life.
—*John 6:63*

Holy Spirit, you are the Spirit of truth, you have come, you guide
me into all truth: for you do not speak of yourself; but whatsoever
you hear, that you speak: and you show me things to come.
—*John 16:13*

I receive power, for the Holy Ghost is come upon me: and I am a
witness unto you, O Lord, both in Jerusalem, and in all Judaea,
and in Samaria, and unto the uttermost part of the earth.
—*Acts 1:8*

That good thing which was committed unto me I
keep by the Holy Ghost which dwells in me.
—*2 Timothy 1:14*

Now the God of hope fill me with all joy and peace in believing, that I may abound in hope, through the power of the Holy Ghost.
—*Romans 15:13*

The blessing of Abraham comes on me through Jesus Christ; I receive the promise of the Spirit through faith.
—*Galatians 3:14*

I receive the Holy Ghost.
—*John 20:22*

Not by works of righteousness which I have done, but according to your mercy you saved me, O Lord, by the washing of regeneration, and renewing of the Holy Ghost.
—*Titus 3:5*

For there are three that bear record in heaven, the Father, the Word, and the Holy Ghost: and you three are one.
—*1 John 5:7*

Christ, you are in me, the body is dead because of sin; but the Spirit is life because of righteousness.
—*Romans 8:10*

The grace of my Lord Jesus Christ, and your love, O God, and the communion of the Holy Ghost, is with me. Amen.
—*2 Corinthians 13:14*

~ 5 ~

Salvation

Thank you, Father, that you are the God of my salvation and you have provided salvation for me through none other than my Lord and Savior, Jesus Christ.

Thank you, Lord Jesus, for the finished work you did through your death, burial, and resurrection. I believe that you died and rose from the dead and I receive your gift of salvation and all that salvation provides. Thank you, Father, that

In you, O God, is my salvation and my glory: the
rock of my strength, and my refuge, is in you.
—*Psalm 62:7*

You, O Lord, are my strength and song, and you are
my salvation: you are my God, and I prepare you an
habitation; you are my father's God, and I exalt you.
—*Exodus 15:2*

For you, O God, so loved the world, that you gave
your only begotten Son, that if I believe in him I
should not perish, but have everlasting life.
—*John 3:16*

I confess with my mouth the Lord Jesus, and I believe in my heart
that you, O God, have raised him from the dead, I am saved.
—*Romans 10:9*

For with my heart I believe unto righteousness; and
with my mouth confession is made unto salvation.
—*Romans 10:10*

You have heard me in a time accepted, O God, and in the
day of salvation have you succoured me: behold, now is
the accepted time; behold, now is the day of salvation.
—*2 Corinthians 6:2*

For by grace am I saved through faith; and that
not of myself: it is your gift, O God.
—*Ephesians 2:8*

For I am not ashamed of the gospel of Christ: for it is the
power of God unto salvation to everyone that believes.
—*Romans 1:16*

I long for your salvation, O Lord; and your law is my delight.
—*Psalm 119:174*

I take the cup of salvation, and I call upon your name, O Lord.
—*Psalm 116:13*

You are the God of my rock, O Lord; in you I trust: you are
my shield, and the horn of my salvation, my high tower,
and my refuge, my saviour; you save me from violence.
—*2 Samuel 22:3*

You have given me the shield of your salvation, O
Lord: and your gentleness has made me great.
—*2 Samuel 22:36*

Lord, you are my rock, and my fortress, and my deliverer;
my God, my strength, in you I trust; my buckler, and
the horn of my salvation, and my high tower.
—*Psalm 18:2*

O Lord, you live; and blessed is my rock; and
exalted is the God of the rock of my salvation.
—2 Samuel 22:47

Behold, you, O God, are my salvation; I trust, and I
am not afraid: for the LORD JEHOVAH is my strength
and my song; you also are my salvation.
—Isaiah 12:2

Wherefore, as I have always obeyed, I work out
my own salvation with fear and trembling.
—Philippians 2:12

I take the helmet of salvation, and the sword of
the Spirit, which is your word, O God.
—Ephesians 6:17

I praise you, O Lord: for you hear me, and you are my salvation.
—Psalm 118:21

I sing unto you, O Lord, I show forth
from day to day your salvation.
—1 Chronicles 16:23

I trust in your mercy; my heart rejoices in your salvation.
—Psalm 13:5

I am kept by your power, O God, through faith unto
salvation ready to be revealed in the last time.
—1 Peter 1:5

I am of the day and I am sober, I put on the breastplate of
faith and love; and for an helmet, the hope of salvation.
—1 Thessalonians 5:8

Not by works of righteousness which I have done, but
according to your mercy you saved me, O Lord, by the
washing of regeneration, and renewing of the Holy Ghost.
—*Titus 3:5*

I rejoice in your salvation, and in your name, O God, I set
up my banners: you, O Lord, fulfil all my petitions.
—*Psalm 20:5*

I rejoice in you, O Lord, I joy in the God of my salvation.
—*Habakkuk 3:18*

You only are my rock and my salvation; you are
my defence; I am not greatly moved.
—*Psalm 62:2*

You, O Lord, are my strength and song, and you are my salvation.
—*Psalm 118:14*

You, O God, are rich in mercy, for your great
love wherewith you loved me.
—*Ephesians 2:4*

Even when I was dead in sins, you, O God, have quickened
me together with Christ, by grace I am saved.
—*Ephesians 2:5*

I look unto you, O Lord; I wait for the God
of my salvation: my God hears me.
—*Micah 7:7*

~ 6 ~

Wisdom and Knowledge

I thank you, Father, that you promised in your word that if I lack wisdom, I can ask it of you and you will give me wisdom liberally and without reproach.

I thank you, Father, that you have given me wisdom and knowledge of your word and your word enlightens my every path.

As I daily partake of your word, I am filled with the knowledge of your will in all wisdom and spiritual understanding. Therefore,

I let the word of Christ dwell in me richly in all wisdom; I
teach and admonish others in psalms and hymns and spiritual
songs, I sing with grace in my heart to you, O Lord.
—*Colossians 3:16*

I attend to your words, O Lord; I incline my ear unto your sayings.
—*Proverbs 4:20*

I let not your words depart from my eyes; I
keep them in the midst of my heart.
—*Proverbs 4:21*

For your words are life unto me, O God, and health to all my flesh.
—*Proverbs 4:22*

I keep my heart with all diligence; for out of it are the issues of life.
—*Proverbs 4:23*

I know the truth, and the truth makes me free.
—John 8:32

Your words were found, and I did eat them; and your
word was unto me the joy and rejoicing of my heart: for
I am called by your name, O Lord God of hosts.
—Jeremiah 15:16

Your word, O Lord, is a lamp unto my
feet and a light unto my path.
—Psalm 119:105

Your word have I hid in my heart, that I might not sin against you.
—Psalm 119:11

I meditate in your precepts, O Lord, and
I have respect unto your ways.
—Psalm 119:15

I delight myself in your statutes: I will not forget your word.
—Psalm 119:16

Father, you instruct me and teach me in the way
which I shall go: you guide me with your eye.
—Psalm 32:8

Lord Jesus, you are the Word and you were made flesh, and
dwelt among us, and we beheld your glory, the glory as of
the only begotten of the Father, full of grace and truth.
—John 1:14

Now I am clean through the word which
you have spoken unto me, O Lord.
—John 15:3

I am filled with the knowledge of your will, O Lord,
in all wisdom and spiritual understanding.
—*Colossians 1:9*

There is a spirit in me: and the inspiration of
the Almighty gives me understanding.
—*Job 32:8*

I do not live by bread alone, but by every word of God.
—*Luke 4:4*

This book of the law shall not depart out of my mouth;
but I meditate therein day and night, that I observe to
do according to all that is written therein: for then I
make my way prosperous, and I have good success.
—*Joshua 1:8*

But the Comforter, which is the Holy Ghost, whom the Father has
sent in your name, Lord Jesus, he teaches me all things, and brings
all things to my remembrance, whatsoever you have said unto me.
—*John 14:26*

The God of my Lord Jesus Christ, the Father of glory, give unto
me the spirit of wisdom and revelation in the knowledge of him.
—*Ephesians 1:17*

The eyes of my understanding are enlightened; that I may
know what is the hope of your calling, O God, and what
the riches of the glory of your inheritance in the saints.
—*Ephesians 1:18*

Lord God, you have given me the tongue of the learned, that I
know how to speak a word in season to him that is weary: you
wake morning by morning, you wake my ear to hear as the learned.
—*Isaiah 50:4*

My heart is comforted, being knit together in
love, and unto all riches of the full assurance of
understanding, to the acknowledgement of your
mystery, O God, and of the Father, and of Christ.
—Colossians 2:2

I am filled with your spirit, O God, in wisdom,
and in understanding, and in knowledge,
and in all manner of workmanship.
—Exodus 31:3

I grow in grace, and in the knowledge of my Lord and Saviour
Jesus Christ. To you be glory both now and for ever. Amen.
—2 Peter 3:18

I incline my ear unto wisdom, and I apply
my heart to understanding.
—Proverbs 2:2

I let my heart retain your words, O Lord: I
keep your commandments, and live.
—Proverbs 4:4

I get wisdom, I get understanding: I forget it not; neither
do I decline from the words of your mouth, O God.
—Proverbs 4:5

Wisdom is the principal thing; therefore I get wisdom:
and with all my getting I get understanding.
—Proverbs 4:7

I walk in wisdom toward them that are
without, redeeming the time.
—Colossians 4:5

Before I call, you answer, O Lord; and
while I am yet speaking, you hear.
—*Isaiah 65:24*

I commit my works unto you, O Lord, and
my thoughts are established.
—*Proverbs 16:3*

I give attendance to reading, to exhortation, to doctrine.
—*1 Timothy 4:13*

O Lord, you have made known unto me the mystery
of your will, according to your good pleasure
which you have purposed in yourself.
—*Ephesians 1:9*

I keep your words, O Lord, and I lay up
your commandments with me.
—*Proverbs 7:1*

I keep your commandments, and live; and
your law as the apple of my eye.
—*Proverbs 7:2*

I bind your words upon my fingers, O Lord, I
write them upon the table of my heart.
—*Proverbs 7:3*

I give all diligence, I add to my faith
virtue; and to virtue knowledge.
—*2 Peter 1:5*

I add to knowledge temperance; and to temperance
patience; and to patience godliness.
—*2 Peter 1:6*

I add to godliness brotherly kindness; and
to brotherly kindness charity.
—*2 Peter 1:7*

These things are in me, and abound, they make
me that I shall neither be barren nor unfruitful in
the knowledge of my Lord Jesus Christ.
—*2 Peter 1:8*

O Lord, the commandment is a lamp; and the law is
light; and reproofs of instruction are the way of life.
—*Proverbs 6:23*

Lord God, the mystery which has been hid from ages and
from generations, is now made manifest to me, your saint.
—*Colossians 1:26*

To me, O God, you make known what is the riches
of the glory of this mystery among the Gentiles;
which is Christ in me, the hope of glory.
—*Colossians 1:27*

Whereunto I also labor, striving according to your
working, Lord Jesus, which works in me mightily.
—*Colossians 1:29*

In you, Jesus Christ, are hid all the treasures
of wisdom and knowledge.
—*Colossians 2:3*

When I go, your commandment leads me, O Lord, when
I sleep, it keeps me, when I awake, it talks with me.
—*Proverbs 6:22*

The entrance of your words gives me light, O Lord;
it gives understanding unto the simple.
—*Psalm 119:130*

As newborn babes, I desire the sincere milk
of the word, that I may grow thereby.
—*1 Peter 2:2*

Your law, O Lord, is perfect, converting my soul: your
testimony, O Lord, is sure, making wise the simple.
—*Psalm 19:7*

Your statutes, O Lord, are right, rejoicing my heart: your
commandment, O Lord, is pure, enlightening my eyes.
—*Psalm 19:8*

The fear of the Lord is clean, enduring forever: your
judgments, O Lord, are true and righteous altogether.
—*Psalm 19:9*

More to be desired are your words than gold, yea, than much
fine gold: sweeter also than honey and the honeycomb.
—*Psalm 19:10*

In every thing I am enriched by you, Jesus Christ,
in all utterance, and in all knowledge.
—*1 Corinthians 1:5*

O Lord, as I abound in every thing, in faith, and utterance,
and knowledge, and in all diligence, and in your love
to me, I see that I abound in this grace also.
—*2 Corinthians 8:7*

I take your yoke upon me, and I learn of you, Lord Jesus; for
you are meek and lowly in heart: and I find rest unto my soul.
—*Matthew 11:29*

Your secret, O Lord, is with me, I fear you;
and you show me your covenant.
—*Psalm 25:14*

I call unto you, O Lord, and you answer me, and show
me great and mighty things, which I know not.
—*Jeremiah 33:3*

I find wisdom and I find life, and I obtain favour of the Lord.
—*Proverbs 8:35*

I do not live by bread alone, but by every word
that proceeds out of your mouth, O God.
—*Matthew 4:4*

My spirit is your candle, O Lord, searching
all the inward parts of the belly.
—*Proverbs 20:27*

So shall your word be that goes forth out of your mouth, Lord God:
it shall not return unto you void, but it shall accomplish that which
you please, and it shall prosper in the thing whereto you sent it.
—*Isaiah 55:11*

~ 7 ~

Joy and Strength

Father, I thank you that this is the day that you have made, and I will rejoice and be glad in it. I daily rejoice in your goodness, in your love, and in your mercy.

When I am weak, then I am strong, for the joy of the Lord is my strength. When I am downhearted, I can rejoice in you, O Lord, for you have given me the garment of praise for the spirit of heaviness. Therefore, this day,

I rejoice in you, O Lord, always: and again I Rejoice.
—*Philippians 4:4*

My heart rejoices in you, O Lord, because
I trust in your holy name.
—*Psalm 33:21*

This day is holy unto you, O Lord: neither am I
sorry; for the joy of the Lord is my strength.
—*Nehemiah 8:10*

You, O Lord, are my light and my salvation; whom shall I fear?
you are the strength of my life; of whom shall I be afraid?
—*Psalm 27:1*

I am strengthened with all might, according to your glorious
power, unto all patience and longsuffering with joyfulness.
—*Colossians 1:11*

Behold, you, O God, are my salvation; I trust, and I
am not afraid: for the LORD JEHOVAH is my strength
and my song; you also are my salvation.
—*Isaiah 12:2*

Therefore with joy I draw water out of the wells of salvation.
—*Isaiah 12:3*

I am strong in you, O Lord, and in the power of your might.
—*Ephesians 6:10*

I can do all things through Christ which strengthens me.
—*Philippians 4:13*

I wait on you, O Lord: I am of good courage, and
you strengthen my heart: I wait on the Lord.
—*Psalm 27:14*

I rejoice in hope; I am patient in tribulation;
I continue instant in prayer.
—*Romans 12:12*

It is you, O God, that gird me with strength,
and make my way perfect.
—*Psalm 18:32*

My mouth is filled with laughter, and my tongue with singing: I
say among the heathen, The Lord has done great things for me.
—*Psalm 126:2*

Whom having not seen, I love; in whom, though
now I see you not, Lord Jesus, yet believing, I
rejoice with joy unspeakable and full of glory.
—*1 Peter 1:8*

I rejoice, inasmuch as I am a partaker of Christ's
sufferings; that, when your glory, O Lord, shall be
revealed, I may be glad also with exceeding joy.
—*1 Peter 4:13*

O Lord, you have made known to me the ways of life;
you make me full of joy with your countenance.
—*Acts 2:28*

By you, Lord Jesus, I have access by faith into this grace
wherein I stand, and I rejoice in hope of your glory, O God.
—*Romans 5:2*

O Lord, your grace is sufficient for me: for your
strength is made perfect in weakness.
—*2 Corinthians 12:9*

I am strong in the grace that is in Christ Jesus.
—*2 Timothy 2:1*

My meditation of you is sweet: I am glad in you, O Lord.
—*Psalm 104:34*

You, O Lord, are my strength and song, and you are
my salvation: you are my God, and I prepare you an
habitation; you are my father's God, and I exalt you.
—*Exodus 15:2*

My spirit rejoices in you, O God my Saviour.
—*Luke 1:47*

My heart is glad, and my glory rejoices: my flesh
also rests in hope.
—*Psalm 16:9*

Now the God of hope fill me with all joy and peace in believing,
that I may abound in hope, through the power of the Holy Ghost.
—*Romans 15:13*

My lips greatly rejoice when I sing unto you, O
Lord; and my soul, which you have redeemed.
—*Psalm 71:23*

O God, you are my strength and power:
and you make my way perfect.
—*2 Samuel 22:33*

O Lord, you grant me, according to the riches of your glory, to
be strengthened with might by your Spirit in my inner man.
—*Ephesians 3:16*

I trust in you, O Lord, forever: for in the LORD
JEHOVAH is everlasting strength.
—*Isaiah 26:4*

~ 8 ~

Peace

I thank you, Father, that you have provided your overwhelming peace for me to walk in and live in. Have you not commanded me to shod my feet with the preparation of the gospel of peace?

I choose to walk in your peace, for your word declares that you will keep me in perfect peace when my mind is stayed on you. Therefore,

I go out with joy, and I am led forth with peace.
—*Isaiah 55:12*

I let your peace, O God, rule in my heart, to the which also I am called in one body; and I am thankful.
—*Colossians 3:15*

Lord, you keep me in perfect peace, because my mind is stayed on you: because I trust in you.
—*Isaiah 26:3*

Peace you leave with me, O Lord, your peace you give unto me: not as the world gives, give you unto me. I let not my heart be troubled, neither do I let it be afraid.
—*John 14:27*

My feet are shod with the preparation of the gospel of peace.
—*Ephesians 6:15*

Lord, you guide my feet into the way of peace.
—*Luke 1:79*

O Lord, you give strength unto me; Lord you bless me with peace.
—Psalm 29:11

For the mountains shall depart, and the hills be removed;
but your kindness shall not depart from me, neither
shall the covenant of your peace be removed.
—Isaiah 54:10

I am careful for nothing; but in everything by
prayer and supplication with thanksgiving I let my
requests be made known unto you, O God.
—Philippians 4:6

And your peace, O God, which passes all understanding,
keeps my heart and mind through Christ Jesus.
—Philippians 4:7

Finally, whatsoever things are true, whatsoever things are honest,
whatsoever things are just, whatsoever things are pure, whatsoever
things are lovely, whatsoever things are of good report; if there
be any virtue, and if there be any praise, I think on these things.
—Philippians 4:8

I have great peace because I love your law:
and nothing shall offend me.
—Psalm 119:165

For you know the thoughts that you think toward me, O Lord,
thoughts of peace, and not of evil, to give me an expected end.
—Jeremiah 29:11

I endeavour to keep the unity of the Spirit in the bond of peace.
—Ephesians 4:3

I depart from evil, and I do good; I seek peace, and I pursue it.
—Psalm 34:14

I hearken to your commandments! therefore my peace is as
a river, and my righteousness as the waves of the sea.
—*Isaiah 48:18*

I acquaint now myself with you, O Lord, and I
am at peace: thereby good comes unto me.
—*Job 22:21*

It is vain for me to rise up early, to sit up late, to eat the bread
of sorrows: I am your beloved and you give me sleep.
—*Psalm 127:2*

Lord, you lift up your countenance upon me, and give me peace.
—*Numbers 6:26*

I hear what God the Lord speaks; for you speak
peace unto me, and to your saints.
—*Psalm 85:8*

Peace is within my walls, and prosperity within my palaces.
—*Psalm 122:7*

The work of my righteousness is peace; and the effect
of righteousness quietness and assurance for ever.
—*Isaiah 32:17*

I dwell in a peaceable habitation, and in sure
dwellings, and in quiet resting places.
—*Isaiah 32:18*

I both lay me down in peace, and sleep: for you,
O Lord, only make me dwell in safety.
—*Psalm 4:8*

When I lie down, I shall not be afraid: yea, I shall
lie down, and my sleep shall be sweet.
—*Proverbs 3:24*

I laid me down and slept; I awaked; for you, O Lord, sustained me.
—*Psalm 3:5*

I awaked, and beheld; and my sleep was sweet unto me.
—*Jeremiah 31:26*

When I go, your commandment leads me, O Lord, when
I sleep, it keeps me, when I awake, it talks with me.
—*Proverbs 6:22*

Grace and peace is multiplied unto me through your
knowledge, O God, and of Jesus my Lord.
—*2 Peter 1:2*

~ 9 ~

Faith

Father, I thank you that you have dealt to me the measure of faith to live by and you desire that I walk and live by faith daily.

You desire that I not only live by faith but that my faith increases and grows daily. Your word declares that faith comes by hearing and hearing by the word of God.

Therefore, as I speak your word, I hear your word, and as I hear your spoken word, it causes my faith to grow and increase continually. Therefore, I declare that

I have faith in you, O God.
—Mark 11:22

I look unto you, Lord Jesus, the author and finisher of my faith.
—Hebrews 12:2

For therein is your righteousness revealed from faith to faith: as it is written, the just shall live by faith, I am just and I live by faith.
—Romans 1:17

Therefore being justified by faith, I have peace with you, O God, through my Lord Jesus Christ.
—Romans 5:1

By you, Lord Jesus, I have access by faith into this grace wherein I stand, and I rejoice in hope of your glory, O God.
—Romans 5:2

Now my faith is the substance of things hoped
for, the evidence of things not seen.
—*Hebrews 11:1*

For by grace am I saved through faith; and that
not of myself: it is your gift, O God.
—*Ephesians 2:8*

The trial of my faith, being much more precious than of gold
that perishes, though it is tried with fire, it is found unto praise
and honour and glory at your appearing, Jesus Christ.
—*1 Peter 1:7*

Through the grace given unto me, I think not of myself more
highly than I ought to think; but I think soberly, according
as you, O God, have dealt to me the measure of faith.
—*Romans 12:3*

The fruit of the Spirit in me is love, joy, peace,
longsuffering, gentleness, goodness, faith, meekness,
temperance: against such there is no law.
—*Galatians 5:22, 23*

I take the shield of faith, wherewith I am able to
quench all the fiery darts of the wicked.
—*Ephesians 6:16*

I call those things which be not as though they were.
—*Romans 4:17*

I trust in you, O Lord, with all my heart; and I
lean not unto my own understanding.
—*Proverbs 3:5*

In all my ways I acknowledge you, O
Lord, and you direct my paths.
—Proverbs 3:6

My faith comes by hearing, and hearing by your word, O God.
—Romans 10:17

I build up myself on my most holy faith, praying in the Holy Ghost.
—Jude 1:20

I stagger not at your promise, O God, through unbelief;
but I am strong in faith, I give glory to God.
—Romans 4:20

I am fully persuaded that, what you have promised,
O God, you are able also to perform.
—Romans 4:21

I say unto this mountain, Be thou removed, and be thou cast
into the sea; and I do not doubt in my heart, but I believe that
those things which I say come to pass; I have whatsoever I say.
—Mark 11:23

What things soever I desire, when I pray, I believe
that I receive them, and I have them.
—Mark 11:24

While I look not at the things which are seen, but at the
things which are not seen: for the things which are seen are
temporal; but the things which are not seen are eternal.
—2 Corinthians 4:18

I receive the end of my faith, even the salvation of my soul.
—1 Peter 1:9

I fight the good fight of faith, I lay hold on eternal
life, whereunto I am also called, and I have professed
a good profession before many witnesses.
—*1 Timothy 6:12*

I walk by faith, not by sight.
—*2 Corinthians 5:7*

My faith does not stand in the wisdom of
men, but in your power, O God.
—*1 Corinthians 2:5*

Father, I draw near with a true heart in full assurance
of faith, having my heart sprinkled from an evil
conscience, and my body washed with pure water.
—*Hebrews 10:22*

In you, Christ Jesus, I have boldness and
access with confidence by your faith.
—*Ephesians 3:12*

I examine myself, whether I am in the faith; I prove my own self.
—*2 Corinthians 13:5*

I hold the mystery of the faith in a pure conscience.
—*1 Timothy 3:9*

I hold fast the profession of my faith without wavering;
(for you, O Lord, are faithful that promised).
—*Hebrews 10:23*

The word is nigh me, even in my mouth, and in my
heart: that is, the word of faith, which I preach.
—*Romans 10:8*

Jesus Christ, you are the same yesterday, and to day, and for ever.
—Hebrews 13:8

I continue in the faith grounded and settled, and I am
not moved away from the hope of the gospel, which
I have heard, and which was preached to me.
—Colossians 1:23

O God, you are able to do exceeding abundantly above all that
I ask or think, according to the power that works in me.
—Ephesians 3:20

Unto you be glory in the church by Christ Jesus
throughout all ages, world without end. Amen.
—Ephesians 3:21

~ 10 ~

Righteousness

Father, you have made me your righteousness in Christ Jesus. Lord Jesus, because of your finished work, I am free from sin and I am your servant of righteousness.

You said in your word that if I hunger and thirst after righteousness, I would be filled. Therefore,

I am filled with the fruits of righteousness, which are by
Jesus Christ, unto your glory and praise, O God.
—*Philippians 1:11*

I believe in you, O Lord; and you counted
it to me for righteousness.
—*Genesis 15:6*

I am the righteousness of God in Christ Jesus because
you, Lord Jesus, who knew no sin became sin for me.
—*2 Corinthians 5:21*

But of you, O God, am I in Christ Jesus, who of God is made unto
me wisdom, and righteousness, and sanctification, and redemption.
—*1 Corinthians 1:30*

For if by one man's offence death reigned by one; much
more I which receive abundance of grace and of the gift of
righteousness shall reign in life by one, Jesus Christ.
—*Romans 5:17*

I am found in you, O Lord, not having mine own righteousness,
which is of the law, but that which is through the faith of
Christ, the righteousness which is of God by faith.
—*Philippians 3:9*

I do hunger and thirst after righteousness: for I am filled.
—*Matthew 5:6*

I yield not my members as instruments of unrighteousness unto
sin: but I yield myself unto you, O God, as being alive from the
dead, and my members as instruments of righteousness unto God.
—*Romans 6:13*

O Lord, you rewarded me according to my righteousness:
according to the cleanness of my hands have you recompensed me.
—*2 Samuel 22:21*

I yield myself a servant of obedience unto righteousness.
—*Romans 6:16*

Being then made free from sin, I became
the servant of righteousness.
—*Romans 6:18*

I yield my members a servant to righteousness unto holiness.
—*Romans 6:19*

I stand therefore, having my loins girt about with truth,
and I have on the breastplate of righteousness.
—*Ephesians 6:14*

The righteousness of the law is fulfilled in me, I
walk not after the flesh, but after the Spirit.
—*Romans 8:4*

I offer unto you, O Lord, an offering in righteousness.
—*Malachi 3:3*

Christ, you are in me, the body is dead because of sin;
but the Spirit is life because of righteousness.
—*Romans 8:10*

I through the Spirit wait for the hope of righteousness by faith.
—*Galatians 5:5*

For with my heart I believe unto righteousness; and
with my mouth confession is made unto salvation.
—*Romans 10:10*

I put on the new man, which after you, O God, is
created in righteousness and true holiness.
—*Ephesians 4:24*

I follow after righteousness, godliness,
faith, love, patience, meekness.
—*1 Timothy 6:11*

I offer the sacrifices of righteousness, and
I put my trust in you, O Lord.
—*Psalm 4:5*

The gates of righteousness are open to me: I go
into them, and I praise you, O Lord.
—*Psalm 118:19*

Lord, your eyes are over the righteous, and
your ears are open unto my prayers.
—*1 Peter 3:12*

The work of my righteousness is peace; and the effect
of righteousness quietness and assurance for ever.
—*Isaiah 32:17*

I praise you, O Lord, according to your righteousness:
and I sing praise to your name, O Lord most High.
—*Psalm 7:17*

Lord, I know that you are righteous, I do
righteousness and I am born of you.
—*1 John 2:29*

I confess my faults to others, and I pray for others, and I am healed.
I am righteous, and my effectual fervent prayer avails much.
—*James 5:16*

I hearken to your commandments! therefore my peace is as
a river, and my righteousness as the waves of the sea.
—*Isaiah 48:18*

Henceforth there is laid up for me a crown of righteousness, which
you, O Lord, my righteous judge, shall give me at that day: and
not to me only, but unto all them also that love your appearing.
—*2 Timothy 4:8*

~ 11 ~

My Identity in Christ

Father, I realize that it is important for me to know who I am in you. Knowing that I am the finished work of Jesus Christ causes me to realize that I am victorious in you.

In you, Lord Jesus, I am more than a conqueror. I am blessed, I am redeemed, I am healed, I am saved, I am filled with the Spirit of God, I am justified, and I am sanctified.

Lord Jesus, I confess that I am all that you created me to become in you. Therefore,

> I am more than a conqueror through you,
> Christ Jesus, that loved me.
> —*Romans 8:37*

I am redeemed from the curse of the law, Christ being made a curse for me: for it is written, cursed is every one that hangs on a tree.
—*Galatians 3:13*

> I am an holy people unto you, O Lord my God, and you
> have chosen me to be a peculiar people unto yourself,
> above all the nations that are upon the earth.
> —*Deuteronomy 14:2*

I am a chosen generation, a royal priesthood, an holy nation, a peculiar people; that I should show forth your praises, O God, who called me out of darkness into your marvellous light.
—*1 Peter 2:9*

I am Christ's, therefore I am Abraham's seed,
and an heir according to the promise.
—*Galatians 3:29*

I am crucified with Christ: nevertheless I live; yet not I, but Christ
lives in me: and the life which I now live in the flesh I live by the
faith of the Son of God, who loved me, and gave himself for me.
—*Galatians 2:20*

I am justified freely by your grace, O God, through
the redemption that is in Christ Jesus.
—*Romans 3:24*

I am rooted and built up in you, O Lord, and I am stablished in the
faith, as I have been taught, abounding therein with thanksgiving.
—*Colossians 2:7*

I am your workmanship, created in Christ Jesus
unto good works, which you, O God, have before
ordained that I should walk in them.
—*Ephesians 2:10*

I am in Christ, I am a new creature: old things are
passed away; behold, all things are become new.
—*2 Corinthians 5:17*

I am blessed with all spiritual blessings
in heavenly places in Christ.
—*Ephesians 1:3*

I am chosen in you, O Lord, before the foundation of the
world, I am holy and without blame before you in love.
—*Ephesians 1:4*

I am predestinated unto the adoption of children by Jesus Christ
to himself, according to the good pleasure of your will, O God.
—Ephesians 1:5

I am accepted in the beloved.
—Ephesians 1:6

I have redemption through your blood, Lord Jesus, the
forgiveness of sins, according to the riches of your grace.
—Ephesians 1:7

I am to the praise of your glory, who first trusted in Christ.
—Ephesians 1:12

I am sealed with that holy Spirit of promise.
—Ephesians 1:13

I am complete in you, O Lord, which is the
head of all principality and power.
—Colossians 2:10

I am the righteousness of God in Christ Jesus because
you, Lord Jesus, who knew no sin became sin for me.
—2 Corinthians 5:21

I am a fool for Christ's sake, but I am wise in Christ.
—1 Corinthians 4:10

I am risen with Christ, I seek those things which are
above, where Christ sits on your right hand, O God.
—Colossians 3:1

I am begotten again unto a lively hope by the
resurrection of Jesus Christ from the dead.
—1 Peter 1:3

I am quickened together with you, Jesus
Christ, by grace I am saved.
—*Ephesians 2:5*

I am raised up together, and I sit together in
heavenly places in Christ Jesus.
—*Ephesians 2:6*

I am an ambassador for Christ, I am reconciled to you, O God.
—*2 Corinthians 5:20*

I am made nigh by the blood of Christ.
—*Ephesians 2:13*

Through you, Lord Jesus, I have access
by one Spirit unto the Father.
—*Ephesians 2:18*

I am no more a stranger and foreigner, but I am a fellow
citizen with the saints, and of the household of God.
—*Ephesians 2:19*

I am built upon the foundation of the apostles and prophets,
Jesus Christ himself being the chief corner stone.
—*Ephesians 2:20*

In you all the building fitly framed together grows
unto an holy temple in you, O Lord.
—*Ephesians 2:21*

In you, Lord Jesus, I also am built together for
an habitation of God through the Spirit.
—*Ephesians 2:22*

I am sanctified in you, Christ Jesus, I am called to be a saint, with all that in every place I call upon the name of Jesus Christ my Lord.
—1 Corinthians 1:2

I am sanctified by you, O God my Father, and I
am preserved in Jesus Christ, and called.
—Jude 1:1

I am your child, O God, by faith in Christ Jesus.
—Galatians 3:26

I am baptized with the Holy Ghost, and with fire.
—Matthew 3:11

I am baptized into Christ and I have put on Christ.
—Galatians 3:27

I am strong in you, O Lord, and in the power of your might.
—Ephesians 6:10

I am strengthened with all might, according to your glorious power, unto all patience and longsuffering with joyfulness.
—Colossians 1:11

I am delivered from the power of darkness, and I am translated into the kingdom of your dear Son, O God.
—Colossians 1:13

In you, Lord Jesus, I have redemption through
your blood, even the forgiveness of sins.
—Colossians 1:14

I am confident of this very thing, that you, O
Lord, who have begun a good work in me will
perform it until the day of Jesus Christ.
—Philippians 1:6

In every thing I am enriched by you, Jesus Christ,
in all utterance, and in all knowledge.
—*1 Corinthians 1:5*

I am confirmed unto the end, that I may be
blameless in the day of my Lord Jesus Christ.
—*1 Corinthians 1:8*

I am a labourer together with you, O God: I am
your husbandry, I am your building.
—*1 Corinthians 3:9*

I am the temple of God, and your Spirit, O God, dwells in me.
—*1 Corinthians 3:16*

In you, O Lord, I am circumcised with the circumcision
made without hands, in putting off the body of the
sins of the flesh by the circumcision of Christ.
—*Colossians 2:11*

I am buried with you, Lord Jesus, in baptism, wherein
also I am risen with you through the faith of the operation
of God, who has raised you from the dead.
—*Colossians 2:12*

I am quickened together with you, Lord Jesus,
you have forgiven me all trespasses.
—*Colossians 2:13*

Therefore being justified by faith, I have peace with
you, O God, through my Lord Jesus Christ.
—*Romans 5:1*

By you, Lord Jesus, I have access by faith into this grace
wherein I stand, and I rejoice in hope of your glory, O God.
—*Romans 5:2*

~ 12 ~

Health and Healing

Thank you, Father, for providing health and healing for my total being. You, O God, are my Jehovah Rapha, the Lord my Healer, and you desire that I daily walk in health in my body and in my soul.

Thank you, Lord Jesus, that you took my infirmities and you bore my sicknesses so that I wouldn't have to bear them.

Father, you said in your word that you would put none of these diseases on me, for you are the Lord who heals me. I thank you, Father, that I don't have to be sick or afflicted. Therefore, I confess that

I am prosperous in all things and in health,
even as my soul prospers.
—*3 John 1:2*

For your words are life unto me, O God, and health to all my flesh.
—*Proverbs 4:22*

Jesus Christ, you are the same yesterday, and to day, and for ever.
—*Hebrews 13:8*

Lord Jesus, surely you have borne my griefs,
and carried my sorrows: yet we did esteem you
stricken, smitten of God, and afflicted.
—*Isaiah 53:4*

But you were wounded for my transgressions, you were
bruised for my iniquities: the chastisement of my peace
was upon you; and with your stripes I am healed.
—*Isaiah 53:5*

Lord Jesus, yourself took my infirmities, and bare my sicknesses.
—*Matthew 8:17*

O Lord, you sent your word, and healed me,
and delivered me from my destructions.
—*Psalm 107:20*

Who your own self bare my sins in your own body on
the tree, Lord Jesus, that I, being dead to sins, should live
unto righteousness: by your stripes I was healed.
—*1 Peter 2:24*

I diligently hearken to your voice, O Lord my God, and I
do that which is right in your sight, and I give ear to your
commandments, and I keep all your statutes, you put none of
these diseases upon me, for you are the Lord that heals me.
—*Exodus 15:26*

I serve you, O Lord my God, and you bless my bread, and my
water; and you take sickness away from the midst of me.
—*Exodus 23:25*

My light breaks forth as the morning, my health
springs forth speedily: and my righteousness goes
before me; your glory, O Lord, is my rereward.
—*Isaiah 58:8*

My merry heart does me good like a medicine.
—*Proverbs 17:22*

Lord, you forgive all my iniquities; you heal all my diseases.
—*Psalm 103:3*

You redeem my life from destruction, O Lord; you
crown me with lovingkindness and tender mercies.
—*Psalm 103:4*

O Lord, you perfect that which concerns me,
your mercy, O Lord, endures forever.
—*Psalm 138:8*

O Lord, you satisfy my mouth with good things;
so that my youth is renewed like the eagle's.
—*Psalm 103:5*

Blessed is the fruit of my body and the fruit of my ground.
—*Deuteronomy 28:4*

Lord, you deliver me out of all my afflictions.
—*Psalm 34:19*

Heal me, O Lord, and I am healed; save me,
and I am saved: for you are my praise.
—*Jeremiah 17:14*

For you, O Lord, restore health unto me,
and you heal me of my wounds.
—*Jeremiah 30:17*

Behold, you bring me health and cure, O Lord, and you cure
me, and reveal unto me the abundance of peace and truth.
—*Jeremiah 33:6*

There shall no evil befall me, neither shall
any plague come nigh my dwelling.
—*Psalm 91:10*

I have power against unclean spirits, to cast them out, and
to heal all manner of sickness and all manner of disease.
—*Matthew 10:1*

The thief comes not, but for to steal, and to kill, and
to destroy: but Lord Jesus, you have come that I might
have life, and that I might have it more abundantly.
—*John 10:10*

My prayer of faith saves the sick, and you, O Lord, shall raise him
up; and if he has committed sins, they shall be forgiven him.
—*James 5:15*

I confess my faults to others, and I pray for others, and I am healed.
I am righteous, and my effectual fervent prayer avails much.
—*James 5:16*

Lord Jesus, your power is present to heal me.
—*Luke 5:17*

I lay hands on the sick, and they recover.
—*Mark 16:18*

With long life you satisfy me, O Lord, and show me your salvation.
—*Psalm 91:16*

Grace and peace is multiplied unto me through your
knowledge, O God, and of Jesus my Lord.
—*2 Peter 1:2*

O God, your divine power has given unto me all things that
pertain unto life and godliness, through the knowledge of
Jesus Christ who has called me to glory and virtue.
—*2 Peter 1:3*

~ 13 ~

Prosperity

Thank you, Father, that you desire that I prosper in every area of my life. You desire that I live on the resources of heaven and that I prosper in my spirit, my soul, and my body.

You are my source, not my job or my possessions. Because I offer unto you my tithes and offerings, you open the windows of heaven unto me and pour me out a blessing I do not have room enough to receive.

As I sow seeds, you continue to give me more seed to sow, so that I can give into every good work. As I yield every part of my being to you, I partake of your divine prosperity.

I confess and I believe that all my needs are supplied according to your riches in glory by Christ Jesus. Therefore,

I seek first your kingdom, O God, and your
righteousness, and all these things are added to me.
—*Matthew 6:33*

I abide in you, Lord Jesus, and your words abide in
me, I ask what I will, and it is done unto me.
—*John 15:7*

You, O God, supply all my need according to
your riches in glory by Christ Jesus.
—*Philippians 4:19*

O Lord, you are my shepherd; I shall not want.
—Psalm 23:1

You prepare a table before me in the presence of mine enemies: you anoint my head with oil; my cup runs over.
—Psalm 23:5

O God, your divine power has given unto me all things that pertain unto life and godliness, through the knowledge of Jesus Christ who has called me to glory and virtue.
—2 Peter 1:3

I delight myself also in you, O Lord, and you give me the desires of my heart.
—Psalm 37:4

You are the Lord, my Redeemer, the Holy One of Israel; you are the Lord my God which teaches me to profit, which leads me by the way that I should go.
—Isaiah 48:17

I seek you, O Lord, and I do not want any good thing.
—Psalm 34:10

I honour you, O Lord, with my substance, and with the firstfruits of all my increase.
—Proverbs 3:9

My barns are filled with plenty, and my presses burst out with new wine.
—Proverbs 3:10

I ask, and it is given me; I seek, and I find; I knock, and it is opened unto me.
—Matthew 7:7

I obey and serve you, O Lord, I spend my days
in prosperity, and my years in pleasures.
—*Job 36:11*

Blessed are you, O Lord, who daily loads me with
benefits, even the God of my salvation.
—*Psalm 68:19*

I remember you, O Lord my God: for it is you that give me
power to get wealth, that you may establish your covenant
which you sware unto my fathers, as it is this day.
—*Deuteronomy 8:18*

And this is the confidence that I have in you, O Lord, that,
if I ask any thing according to your will, you hear me.
—*1 John 5:14*

And if I know that you hear me, whatsoever I ask, I
know that I have the petitions that I desired of you.
—*1 John 5:15*

I owe no man any thing, but to love them: for
in loving others, I fulfill the law.
—*Romans 13:8*

I give, and it is given unto me; good measure, pressed
down, and shaken together, and running over, men
give into my bosom. For with the same measure
that I mete withal it is measured to me again.
—*Luke 6:38*

I hearken diligently unto your voice, O Lord my God,
to observe and to do all your commandments which
you command me this day, that you, O Lord my God,
set me on high above all nations of the earth.
—*Deuteronomy 28:1*

And all these blessings come on me, and overtake me,
because I hearken unto your voice, O Lord my God.
—Deuteronomy 28:2

I am blessed in the city, and I am blessed in the field.
—Deuteronomy 28:3

Blessed is the fruit of my body, and the fruit of
my ground, and the fruit of my cattle, the increase
of my kine, and the flocks of my sheep.
—Deuteronomy 28:4

Blessed is my basket and my store.
—Deuteronomy 28:5

I am blessed when I come in, and I am blessed when I go out.
—Deuteronomy 28:6

O Lord, you cause my enemies that rise up against
me to be smitten before my face: they shall come out
against me one way, and flee before me seven ways.
—Deuteronomy 28:7

O Lord, you command the blessing upon me in my
storehouses, and in all that I set my hand unto; and you bless
me in the land which you, O Lord my God, give me.
—Deuteronomy 28:8

Lord, you establish me an holy people unto yourself, as you
have sworn unto me, because I keep your commandments,
O Lord my God, and I walk in your ways.
—Deuteronomy 28:9

And all people of the earth shall see that I am called by
your name, O Lord; and they shall be afraid of me.
—Deuteronomy 28:10

And you, O Lord, make me plenteous in
goods, in the fruit of my body.
—*Deuteronomy 28:11*

O Lord, you open unto me your good treasure, the heaven to
give rain unto my land in your season, and to bless all the work
of my hand: and I lend unto many nations, and I do not borrow.
—*Deuteronomy 28:12*

Lord, you make me the head, and not the tail; and I am
above only, and I am not beneath; because I hearken
unto your commandments, O Lord my God, which you
command me this day, to observe and to do them.
—*Deuteronomy 28:13*

And I do not go aside from any of the words which
you command me this day, to the right hand, or to
the left, to go after other gods to serve them.
—*Deuteronomy 28:14*

I bring all my tithes into the storehouse, that there may be meat
in your house, and I prove you now herewith, O Lord of hosts,
that you open me the windows of heaven, and pour me out a
blessing, that there shall not be room enough to receive it.
—*Malachi 3:10*

And you rebuke the devourer for my sake, and he shall not
destroy the fruits of my ground; neither shall my vine cast
her fruit before the time in the field, O Lord of hosts.
—*Malachi 3:11*

I sow bountifully, I reap also bountifully.
—*2 Corinthians 9:6*

According as I purpose in my heart, so I give; not grudgingly,
or of necessity: for you, O God, love a cheerful giver.
—*2 Corinthians 9:7*

And you, O God, make all grace abound toward
me; that I, always having all sufficiency in all
things, may abound to every good work.
—*2 Corinthians 9:8*

Peace is within my walls, and prosperity within my palaces.
—*Psalm 122:7*

And all things, whatsoever I ask in prayer, believing, I receive.
—*Matthew 21:22*

Wisdom and knowledge is granted unto me, O Lord;
and you give me riches, and wealth, and honour.
—*2 Chronicles 1:12*

I keep therefore the words of your covenant, O Lord,
and I do them, that I may prosper in all that I do.
—*Deuteronomy 29:9*

You, O Lord, that minister seed to the sower both
minister bread for my food, and multiply my seed
sown, and increase the fruits of my righteousness.
—*2 Corinthians 9:10*

I am enriched in every thing to all bountifulness, which
causes through me thanksgiving to you, O God.
—*2 Corinthians 9:11*

Wealth and riches are in my house: and my
righteousness endures for ever.
—*Psalm 112:3*

You, O God, give me riches and wealth, and you give
me power to eat thereof, and to take my portion, and
to rejoice in my labor; this is your gift, O God.
—*Ecclesiastes 5:19*

I am careful for nothing; but in everything by
prayer and supplication with thanksgiving I let my
requests be made known unto you, O God.
—*Philippians 4:6*

I am like a tree planted by the rivers of water, that
brings forth my fruit in my season; my leaf also shall
not wither; and whatsoever I do prospers.
—*Psalm 1:3*

I study to be quiet, and I do my own business,
and I work with my own hands.
—*1 Thessalonians 4:11*

I walk honestly toward them that are without,
and I have lack of nothing.
—*1 Thessalonians 4:12*

Your blessing, O Lord, it makes me rich,
and you add no sorrow with it.
—*Proverbs 10:22*

I shout for joy, and I am glad, I favour your righteous
cause: yea, I say continually, O Lord, be magnified, you
have pleasure in the prosperity of your servant.
—*Psalm 35:27*

The blessing of Abraham comes on me through Jesus
Christ; I receive the promise of the Spirit through faith.
—*Galatians 3:14*

For when you, O God, made promise to Abraham, because
you could swear by no greater, you sware by yourself.
—*Hebrews 6:13*

Saying, Surely blessing you bless me, and
multiplying you multiply me.
—*Hebrews 6:14*

O God, you are able to do exceeding abundantly above all that
I ask or think, according to the power that works in me.
—*Ephesians 3:20*

Unto you be glory in the church by Christ Jesus
throughout all ages, world without end. Amen.
—*Ephesians 3:21*

O Lord, you grant me according to mine own
heart, and fulfil all my counsel.
—*Psalm 20:4*

I rejoice in your salvation, and in your name, O God, I set
up my banners: you, O Lord, fulfil all my petitions.
—*Psalm 20:5*

I leave an inheritance to my children's children:
and the wealth of the sinner is laid up for me.
—*Proverbs 13:22*

I am prosperous in all things and in health,
even as my soul prospers.
—*3 John 1:2*

I find out knowledge of witty inventions.
—*Proverbs 8:12*

Riches and honour are with me; yea,
durable riches and righteousness.
—*Proverbs 8:18*

My fruit is better than gold, O Lord, yea, than fine
gold; and my revenue than choice silver.
—*Proverbs 8:19*

I love wisdom and I inherit substance;
and my treasures are full.
—*Proverbs 8:21*

What things soever I desire, when I pray, I believe
that I receive them, and I have them.
—*Mark 11:24*

And when I stand praying, I forgive, if I have ought
against any: that you, my Father, also which is
in heaven may forgive me my trespasses.
—*Mark 11:25*

I give thanks unto you, Father, which have made me meet
to be a partaker of the inheritance of the saints in light.
—*Colossians 1:12*

O Lord, you perfect that which concerns me,
your mercy, O Lord, endures forever.
—*Psalm 138:8*

For as the rain comes down, and the snow from heaven, and
returns not there, but waters the earth, and makes it bring forth
and bud, that it may give seed to the sower, and bread to the eater.
—*Isaiah 55:10*

So shall your word be that goes forth out of your mouth,
Lord God: it shall not return unto you void, but it
shall accomplish that which you please, and it shall
prosper in the thing whereto you sent it.
—Isaiah 55:11

~ 14 ~

Patience and Rest

Father, you desire that I live my life in patience and that I learn to rest in you. Living in patience causes me to stablish my heart, possess my soul, and inherit the promises of your word.

I choose to rest in you and not fret about the things of this world or the things going on in my life. As I wait and rest in you, I renew my strength, so that I may finish the course that you have set for me in this earth. Therefore,

I let patience have her perfect work, that I may
be perfect and entire, wanting nothing.
—James 1:4

I add to knowledge temperance; and to temperance
patience; and to patience godliness.
—2 Peter 1:6

I will not be weary in well doing: for in due
season I shall reap, if I faint not.
—Galatians 6:9

In my patience I possess my soul.
—Luke 21:19

If I hope for that I see not, then do I with patience wait for it.
—Romans 8:25

For whatsoever things were written aforetime were
written for my learning, that I through patience and
comfort of the scriptures might have hope.
—Romans 15:4

I am patient therefore, unto your coming, O Lord. Behold, the
husbandman waits for the precious fruit of the earth, and have
long patience for it, until you receive the early and latter rain.
—James 5:7

I am not slothful, but I am a follower of them who
through faith and patience inherit the promises.
—Hebrews 6:12

Wherefore seeing I also am compassed about with so
great a cloud of witnesses, I lay aside every weight,
and the sin which does so easily beset me, and I run
with patience the race that is set before me.
—Hebrews 12:1

For I have need of patience, that, after I have done
your will, O God, I receive the promise.
—Hebrews 10:36

I count it all joy when I fall into divers temptations.
—James 1:2

Knowing this, that the trying of my faith works patience.
—James 1:3

I rejoice in hope; I am patient in tribulation;
I continue instant in prayer.
—Romans 12:12

I rest in you, O Lord, and I wait patiently for you: I fret not myself because of him who prospers in his way, because of the man who brings wicked devices to pass.
—Psalm 37:7

I am also patient; I stablish my heart: for
your coming, O Lord, draws nigh.
—James 5:8

I am swift to hear, I am slow to speak, I am slow to wrath.
—James 1:19

Your presence goes with me, O Lord, and you give me rest.
—Exodus 33:14

I glory in tribulations also: knowing that
tribulation works patience in me.
—Romans 5:3

And patience works experience in me; and
experience works hope in me.
—Romans 5:4

I wait upon you, O Lord, and I renew my strength;
I mount up with wings as eagles; I run, and I am
not weary; and I walk, and I do not faint.
—Isaiah 40:31

My heart is glad, and my glory rejoices:
my flesh also rests in hope.
—Psalm 16:9

I stand in awe, and I sin not: I commune with my
own heart upon my bed, and I am still.
—*Psalm 4:4*

I am still, and I know that you are God: you are exalted
among the heathen, and you are exalted in the earth.
—*Psalm 46:10*

~ 15 ~

Meditation and Mind Renewal

Father, you desire that I daily saturate my spirit and my mind with your word so that I will live in the peace that you have provided for me.

Your word declares that out of the abundance of the heart, the mouth speaks. I choose to daily fill my spirit and my mind with your word, so that my mouth will speak faith and not doubt, joy and not sorrow, and peace and not confusion. Therefore,

I put on the new man, which is renewed in knowledge
after the image of him that created me.
—*Colossians 3:10*

I let this mind be in me, which was also in you, Christ Jesus.
—*Philippians 2:5*

I am not conformed to this world: but I am transformed
by the renewing of my mind, that I may prove what is
that good, and acceptable, and perfect, will of God.
—*Romans 12:2*

I cast down imaginations, and every high thing that exalts
itself against the knowledge of God, and I bring into
captivity every thought to the obedience of Christ.
—*2 Corinthians 10:5*

I let no corrupt communication proceed out of my
mouth, but that which is good to the use of edifying,
that it may minister grace unto the hearers.
—*Ephesians 4:29*

This book of the law shall not depart out of my mouth; but
I meditate therein day and night, that I may observe to do
according to all that is written therein: for then I shall make
my way prosperous, and then I shall have good success.
—*Joshua 1:8*

I gird up the loins of my mind, I am sober, and I
hope to the end for the grace that is to be brought
unto me at the revelation of Jesus Christ.
—*1 Peter 1:13*

I put away from me a froward mouth, and
perverse lips I put far from me.
—*Proverbs 4:24*

I ponder the path of my feet, and I let all my ways be established.
—*Proverbs 4:26*

I commit my works unto you, O Lord, and
my thoughts are established.
—*Proverbs 16:3*

I seek not what I shall eat, or what I shall
drink, neither am I of a doubtful mind.
—*Luke 12:29*

For you, O God, have not given me the spirit of fear;
but of power, and of love, and of a sound mind.
—*2 Timothy 1:7*

I thank you, O God, through Jesus Christ my Lord,
that with the mind I myself serve the law of God.
—*Romans 7:25*

I am not soon shaken in mind, or am I troubled, neither by spirit,
nor by word, nor by letter, as that the day of Christ is at hand.
—*2 Thessalonians 2:2*

Mine eyes prevent the night watches, that I
might meditate in your word, O Lord.
—*Psalm 119:148*

I am careful for nothing; but in everything by
prayer and supplication with thanksgiving I let my
requests be made known unto you, O God.
—*Philippians 4:6*

And your peace, O God, which passes all understanding,
keeps my heart and mind through Christ Jesus.
—*Philippians 4:7*

Finally, whatsoever things are true, whatsoever things are honest,
whatsoever things are just, whatsoever things are pure, whatsoever
things are lovely, whatsoever things are of good report; if there
be any virtue, and if there be any praise, I think on these things.
—*Philippians 4:8*

I pray with the spirit, and I pray with the understanding also: I
sing with the spirit, and I sing with the understanding also.
—*1 Corinthians 14:15*

I walk not in the counsel of the ungodly, I stand not in the
way of sinners, I sit not in the seat of the scornful.
—*Psalm 1:1*

My delight is in your law, O Lord; and in your
law do I meditate day and night.
—*Psalm 1:2*

I remember you, O Lord, upon my bed, and I
meditate on you in the night watches.
—*Psalm 63:6*

I meditate also of all your work, and I talk of your doings.
—*Psalm 77:12*

I meditate in your precepts, O Lord, and
I have respect unto your ways.
—*Psalm 119:15*

My hands also I lift up unto your commandments, O
Lord, which I love; and I meditate in your statutes.
—*Psalm 119:48*

I have the mind of Christ.
—*1 Corinthians 2:16*

I am renewed in the spirit of my mind.
—*Ephesians 4:23*

I meditate upon these things; I give myself wholly
to them; that my profiting may appear to all.
—*1 Timothy 4:15*

My mouth speaks of wisdom; and the meditation
of my heart is of understanding.
—*Psalm 49:3*

My meditation of you is sweet: I am glad in you, O Lord.
—*Psalm 104:34*

O how I love your law, O Lord! It is my meditation all the day.
—*Psalm 119:97*

Let the words of my mouth, and the meditation of my heart, be acceptable in your sight, O Lord, my strength, and my redeemer.
—*Psalm 19:14*

~ 16 ~

Sanctification

Father, before the foundations of the world were framed, you knew me and you set me apart for yourself and for your glory.

Thank you, O God, for choosing me, for sanctifying me, and for washing me with the water of your word. Thank you for preserving me unto the coming of my Lord and Savior, Jesus Christ.

Thank you for presenting me unto yourself a glorious church not having spot or wrinkle, holy and without blemish. Therefore,

I am sanctified and cleansed with the
washing of water by the word.
—*Ephesians 5:26*

I am an holy people unto you, O Lord my God: you
have chosen me to be a special people unto yourself,
above all people that are upon the face of the earth.
—*Deuteronomy 7:6*

I am godly, and you have set me apart for yourself,
O Lord: and you hear when I call unto you.
—*Psalm 4:3*

You are the very God of peace, and you sanctify me
wholly; and my whole spirit and soul and body is preserved
blameless unto your coming, O Lord Jesus Christ.
—*1 Thessalonians 5:23*

I sanctify you, O Lord God, in my heart: and I am ready
always to give an answer to every man that asks me a
reason of the hope that is in me with meekness and fear.
—1 Peter 3:15

I am bound to give thanks always to you, O God, because
you have from the beginning chosen me to salvation through
sanctification of the Spirit and belief of the truth.
—2 Thessalonians 2:13

I am sanctified through your truth, O Lord; your word is truth.
—John 17:17

I am sanctified through the offering of your
body, Jesus Christ, once for all.
—Hebrews 10:10

I am washed, I am sanctified, I am justified in your
name, Lord Jesus, and by the Spirit of God.
—1 Corinthians 6:11

I sanctify myself therefore, and I am holy:
for you are the Lord my God.
—Leviticus 20:7

I keep your statutes, and I do them: you
are the Lord which sanctify me.
—Leviticus 20:8

This is your will, O God, even my sanctification,
that I abstain from fornication.
—1 Thessalonians 4:3

I know how to possess my vessel in sanctification and honour.
—1 Thessalonians 4:4

I purge myself from dishonourable things, I am a vessel
unto honour, sanctified, and meet for the master's
use, and prepared unto every good work.
—*2 Timothy 2:21*

I am commended to you, O God, and to the word
of your grace, which builds me up, and gives me an
inheritance among them which are sanctified.
—*Acts 20:32*

I am sanctified in you, Christ Jesus, I am called to be a saint, with
all that in every place I call upon the name of Jesus Christ my Lord.
—*1 Corinthians 1:2*

I am sanctified by the word of God and prayer.
—*1 Timothy 4:5*

But of you, O God, am I in Christ Jesus, who of God is made unto
me wisdom, and righteousness, and sanctification, and redemption.
—*1 Corinthians 1:30*

I keep the sabbath day to sanctify it, as you, O
Lord my God, have commanded me.
—*Deuteronomy 5:12*

For you are the Lord my God: I therefore sanctify
myself, and I am holy; for you, O Lord, are holy.
—*Leviticus 11:44*

I am sanctified by you, O God my Father, and I
am preserved in Jesus Christ, and called.
—*Jude 1:1*

I am sanctified, and by one offering you, Lord
Jesus, have perfected me forever.
—*Hebrews 10:14*

~ 17 ~

Grace

Thank you, Father, for giving me your abundant grace that enables me to walk in the paths you have set before me and to do all you have called and anointed me to do.

Thank you, O God, that you have also made all grace abound toward me, so that I will have all sufficiency in all things and so that I may have an abundance for every good work. Therefore,

I am justified freely by your grace, O God, through
the redemption that is in Christ Jesus.
—*Romans 3:24*

By you, Lord Jesus, I have access by faith into this grace
wherein I stand, and I rejoice in hope of your glory, O God.
—*Romans 5:2*

Therefore it is of faith, that it might be by grace; to the
end the promise might be sure to all the seed; not to
that only which is of the law, but to that also which is of
the faith of Abraham; who is the father of us all.
—*Romans 4:16*

I am not carried about with divers and strange doctrines. For it is a
good thing that my heart is established with grace; not with meats,
which have not profited them that have been occupied therein.
—*Hebrews 13:9*

O God, you make all grace abound toward
me; that I, always having all sufficiency in all
things, may abound to every good work.
—*2 Corinthians 9:8*

Of your fulness, O Lord, have I received, and grace for grace.
—*John 1:16*

For the law was given by Moses, but grace
and truth came by you, Jesus Christ.
—*John 1:17*

I am commended to you, O God, and to the word
of your grace, which builds me up, and gives me an
inheritance among them which are sanctified.
—*Acts 20:32*

For if by one man's offence death reigned by one; much
more I which receive abundance of grace and of the gift of
righteousness shall reign in life by one, Jesus Christ.
—*Romans 5:17*

Moreover the law entered, that the offence might abound.
But where sin abounded, grace did much more abound.
—*Romans 5:20*

As sin has reigned unto death, even so might grace reign through
righteousness unto eternal life by Jesus Christ my Lord.
—*Romans 5:21*

Now my Lord Jesus Christ himself, and God, even
my Father, you have loved me, and have given me
everlasting consolation and good hope through grace.
—*2 Thessalonians 2:16*

Through the grace given unto me, I think not of myself more
highly than I ought to think; but I think soberly, according
as you, O God, have dealt to me the measure of faith.
—*Romans 12:3*

I have then gifts differing according to the grace
that is given to me, whether prophecy, I prophesy
according to the proportion of faith.
—*Romans 12:6*

Grace be unto me, and peace, from God my
Father, and from my Lord Jesus Christ.
—*1 Corinthians 1:3*

For all things are for my sake, that the abundant grace might
through the thanksgiving of many redound to your glory, O God.
—*2 Corinthians 4:15*

For I know your grace, O Lord Jesus Christ, that,
though you were rich, yet for my sake you became
poor, that I through your poverty might be rich.
—*2 Corinthians 8:9*

O Lord, your grace is sufficient for me: for your
strength is made perfect in weakness.
—*2 Corinthians 12:9*

Father, in the ages to come you show the exceeding riches of
your grace in your kindness toward me through Christ Jesus.
—*Ephesians 2:7*

In you I have redemption through your blood, Lord Jesus, the
forgiveness of sins, according to the riches of your grace.
—*Ephesians 1:7*

Even when I was dead in sins, you, O God, have quickened
me together with Christ, by grace I am saved.
—*Ephesians 2:5*

For by grace am I saved through faith; and that
not of myself: it is your gift, O God.
—*Ephesians 2:8*

Wherefore I receive a kingdom which cannot be
moved, I have grace, whereby I serve you, O God,
acceptably with reverence and godly fear.
—*Hebrews 12:28*

Unto me is given grace according to the
measure of the gift of Christ.
—*Ephesians 4:7*

Grace is with me because I love my Lord
Jesus Christ in sincerity. Amen.
—*Ephesians 6:24*

I let my speech be always with grace, seasoned with salt,
that I may know how I ought to answer every man.
—*Colossians 4:6*

I am justified by your grace, O Lord, I am made
an heir according to the hope of eternal life.
—*Titus 3:7*

I come boldly unto your throne of grace, O Lord, that I may
obtain mercy, and find grace to help in time of need.
—*Hebrews 4:16*

Sin does not have dominion over me: for I am
not under the law, but under grace.
—*Romans 6:14*

I look diligent lest I fail of your grace, O God; lest any root of
bitterness springing up trouble me, and thereby many be defiled.
—Hebrews 12:15

But you give more grace. Wherefore you say, O God,
you resist the proud, but give grace unto the humble.
—James 4:6

Lord, you make your face shine upon me,
and you are gracious unto me.
—Numbers 6:25

I gird up the loins of my mind, I am sober, and I
hope to the end for the grace that is to be brought
unto me at the revelation of Jesus Christ.
—1 Peter 1:13

O Lord, as I abound in every thing, in faith, and utterance,
and knowledge, and in all diligence, and in your love
to me, I see that I abound in this grace also.
—2 Corinthians 8:7

Grace and peace is multiplied unto me through your
knowledge, O God, and of Jesus my Lord.
—2 Peter 1:2

I grow in grace, and in the knowledge of my Lord and Saviour
Jesus Christ. To you be glory both now and for ever. Amen.
—2 Peter 3:18

The grace of my Lord Jesus Christ, and your love, O God,
and the communion of the Holy Ghost, is with me. Amen.
—2 Corinthians 13:14

~ 18 ~

Walking in Love

Father, you said in your word that a new commandment has been given unto us: that we love one another. As you have loved us, we should also love one another.

This subject is so important that you decided to make it a commandment. I choose to walk in love so that I can have constant fellowship with you and my fellow man.

If I cannot love my sisters and brothers in you, O Lord, then I have no fellowship with you. Therefore,

I walk in love, as Christ also has loved me, and has
given himself for me an offering and a sacrifice
to you, O God, for a sweetsmelling savour.
—*Ephesians 5:2*

A new commandment you give unto me that I love others;
as you have loved me, O Lord, that I also love others.
—*John 13:34*

By this shall all men know that I am your
disciple, if I have love for others.
—*John 13:35*

I love you, O Lord my God, with all my heart, and
with all my soul, and with all my mind, and with all
my strength: this is the first commandment.
—*Mark 12:30*

And the second is like, namely this, that I love my neighbor as myself. There is none other commandment greater than these.
—*Mark 12:31*

I love not in word, neither in tongue; but in deed and in truth.
—*1 John 3:18*

For in you, Jesus Christ, neither circumcision avails any thing, nor uncircumcision; but my faith which works by love.
—*Galatians 5:6*

I put on therefore, as the elect of God, holy and beloved, bowels of mercies, kindness, humbleness of mind, meekness, longsuffering.
—*Colossians 3:12*

I let my love be without dissimulation. I abhor that which is evil; I cleave to that which is good.
—*Romans 12:9*

Christ, you dwell in my heart by faith; and I am rooted and grounded in love.
—*Ephesians 3:17*

I know the love of Christ, which passes knowledge, and I am filled with all your fulness, O God.
—*Ephesians 3:19*

Lord, you make me to increase and abound in love toward others, and toward all men, even as I do toward you.
—*1 Thessalonians 3:12*

To the end you stablish my heart unblameable in holiness before you, O God, even my Father, at the coming of my Lord Jesus Christ with all your saints.
—*1 Thessalonians 3:13*

I forbear others, and I forgive others, if any man have a
quarrel against me: even as Christ forgave me, so also do I.
—*Colossians 3:13*

And above all these things, I put on charity,
which is the bond of perfectness.
—*Colossians 3:14*

I consider others to provoke unto love and to good works.
—*Hebrews 10:24*

I let my speech be always with grace, seasoned with salt,
that I may know how I ought to answer every man.
—*Colossians 4:6*

I love others: for love is of God; I love and I
am born of God, and I know God.
—*1 John 4:7*

In this was manifested your love, O God, toward
me, because that you sent your only begotten Son
into the world, that I might live through him.
—*1 John 4:9*

Herein is love, not that I loved you, O God, but that you loved
me, and sent your Son to be the propitiation for my sins.
—*1 John 4:10*

I am your beloved, O God, if you so loved
me, I ought also to love others.
—*1 John 4:11*

No one has seen you at any time, O God. If I love others,
you dwell in me, and your love is perfected in me.
—*1 John 4:12*

Hereby I know that I dwell in you, O God, and you in
me, because you have given me of your Spirit.
—*1 John 4:13*

I know and believe the love that you have to me, O God. You are
love, and because I dwell in love I dwell in you, and you in me.
—*1 John 4:16*

Herein is my love made perfect, that I may have boldness in the
day of judgment: because as you are, O God, so am I in this world.
—*1 John 4:17*

There is no fear in my love; but perfect love casts out fear.
—*1 John 4:18*

I love you, O God, because you first loved me.
—*1 John 4:19*

If I say, I love you, O God, and hate my brother, I am
a liar: for if I love not my brother whom I have seen,
how can I love you, O God, whom I have not seen?
—*1 John 4:20*

And this commandment have I from you, That I
love you, O God, and I love my brother also.
—*1 John 4:21*

I am kind to others, tenderhearted, forgiving others, even
as you, O God, for Christ's sake have forgiven me.
—*Ephesians 4:32*

I speak the truth in love, I grow up into you in
all things, which is the head, even Christ.
—*Ephesians 4:15*

I purify my soul in obeying the truth through the
Spirit unto unfeigned love of the brethren, I see
that I love others with a pure heart fervently.
   —1 Peter 1:22

I keep myself in your love, O God, looking for the
mercy of my Lord Jesus Christ unto eternal life.
   —Jude 1:21

Though I speak with the tongues of men and of angels, and have
not charity, I am become as sounding brass, or a tinkling cymbal.
   —1 Corinthians 13:1

And though I have the gift of prophecy, and understand all
mysteries, and all knowledge; and though I have all faith, so that
I could remove mountains, and have not charity, I am nothing.
   —1 Corinthians 13:2

And though I bestow all my goods to feed the
poor, and though I give my body to be burned,
and have not charity, it profits me nothing.
   —1 Corinthians 13:3

My charity suffers long, and is kind; my charity envies
not; my charity vaunts not itself, is not puffed up.
   —1 Corinthians 13:4

My charity does not behave itself unseemly, seeks not
her own, is not easily provoked, thinks no evil.
   —1 Corinthians 13:5

My charity rejoices not in iniquity, but rejoices in the truth.
   —1 Corinthians 13:6

My charity bears all things, believes all things,
hopes all things, endures all things.
—*1 Corinthians 13:7*

My charity never fails.
—*1 Corinthians 13:8*

And now abides faith, hope, charity, these three;
but the greatest of these is charity.
—*1 Corinthians 13:13*

And when I stand praying, I forgive, if I have ought
against any: that you, my Father, also which is
in heaven may forgive me my trespasses.
—*Mark 11:25*

With all lowliness and meekness, with
longsuffering, I forbear others in love.
—*Ephesians 4:2*

I endeavour to keep the unity of the Spirit in the bond of peace.
—*Ephesians 4:3*

You direct my heart into your love, O God,
and into the patient waiting for Christ.
—*2 Thessalonians 3:5*

I let all my things be done with charity.
—*1 Corinthians 16:14*

My love abounds yet more and more in
knowledge and in all judgment.
—*Philippians 1:9*

I approve things that are excellent; that I may be
sincere and without offence till the day of Christ.
—*Philippians 1:10*

I am filled with the fruits of righteousness, which are by
Jesus Christ, unto your glory and praise, O God.
—*Philippians 1:11*

My Confession of Love and Forgiveness

Father, I forgive _____ for the hurt and pain they have caused me.
They have hurt me tremendously. I choose to forgive them, and I
choose to forget the wrong they rendered to me.

Father, because you have forgiven me my trespasses and you
remember them no more, I also forgive _____ their trespasses and
I forget the wrong done against me.

I realize that forgiveness is not a feeling but a decision. I do not feel
like I have forgiven _____ because I still hurt, but I know I have
forgiven them because I choose to forgive them. Father, if I choose
not to forgive _____, I realize that this unforgiveness will separate
me from fellowshipping with you.

So I have decided not to allow anyone or anything to steal my peace,
rob me of my joy, and cause me to walk in strife or unforgiveness. I
will not be afraid to love _____. I will love them with your love, O
God, for your word declares in 1 John 4:18, "There is no fear in love;
but perfect love casts out fear."

Help me to let go of the past and the things that have hurt me. Your word says in Philippians 3:13 and 14, "Brethren, I count not myself to have apprehended: but this one thing I do, forgetting those things which are behind, and reaching forth unto those things which are before, I press toward the mark for the prize of the high calling of God in Christ Jesus."

I let go of the things that have hurt me and held me bound and captive. I choose not to be offended by people's actions or words. Every day and every minute of my life, I choose to walk in the freedom you have provided for me to walk in and live in, O Lord.

Your word declares in John 8:36, "If the Son therefore shall make you free, you shall be free indeed." I declare that I am free in you, O God. Amen!

~ 19 ~

Wives' Confessions

Thank you, Father, for giving me a man after your own heart. A man who seeks after your will for his life, for me, and for our marriage.

Thank you that he covers me with his love and with your word. He protects me and provides for me. As his wife, I choose to submit myself to my husband as unto you, O Lord.

I adorn myself with a meek and quiet spirit, and I live to show love and compassion to him. I reverence my husband, and I abide with him in peace.

I cover my beloved husband with my prayers and with my love that we may experience your love and walk in your divine purpose for our lives. Therefore, O Lord,

I submit myself unto my own husband, as it is fit in you, O Lord.
—*Colossians 3:18*

I am in subjection to my own husband; that, if any obey not the word, they also may without the word be won by my conversation.
—*1 Peter 3:1*

I let not my adorning be that outward adorning of plaiting my hair, and of wearing of gold, or of putting on of apparel.
—*1 Peter 3:3*

But I let my adorning be the hidden man of my heart, in that
which is not corruptible, even the ornament of a meek and
quiet spirit, which is in your sight, O God, of great price.
—1 Peter 3:4

For after this manner I adorn myself, I am in
subjection unto my own husband.
—1 Peter 3:5

I dwell in a peaceful habitation with my husband, and
in sure dwellings, and in quiet resting places.
—Isaiah 32:18

My husband and I are of one mind, we have compassion one of
another, we love as brethren, we are pitiful, we are courteous.
—1 Peter 3:8

My husband and I do not render evil for evil, or railing
for railing: but contrariwise blessing; knowing that we are
thereunto called, that we should inherit a blessing.
—1 Peter 3:9

Lord, you grant me to find rest, in the house of my husband.
—Ruth 1:9

I am a wise woman and I build my house.
—Proverbs 14:1

I depart not from my husband.
—1 Corinthians 7:10

I live joyfully with my husband whom I love
all the days of my life.
—Ecclesiastes 9:9

I render unto my husband due benevolence.
—*1 Corinthians 7:3*

I have not power of my own body, but my husband.
—*1 Corinthians 7:4*

I defraud not my husband, except it be with consent
for a time, that I may give myself to fasting and
prayer; and we come together again.
—*1 Corinthians 7:5*

I love my husband, and I am not bitter against him.
—*Colossians 3:19*

O Lord, you keep my husband in perfect peace, because
his mind is stayed on you, because he trusts in you.
—*Isaiah 26:3*

Blessed are you, O Lord, who daily loads my husband
with benefits, even the God of his salvation.
—*Psalm 68:19*

My husband is strong in you, O Lord, and
in the power of your might.
—*Ephesians 6:10*

My husband and I submit ourselves to
one another in the fear of God.
—*Ephesians 5:21*

I submit myself unto my own husband, as unto you, O Lord.
—*Ephesians 5:22*

I teach the young women to be sober, to love
their husbands, to love their children.
—*Titus 2:4*

I am a virtuous woman, for my price is far above rubies.
—*Proverbs 31:10*

The heart of my husband does safely trust in me,
so that he shall have no need of spoil.
—*Proverbs 31:11*

I do my husband good and not evil all the days of my life.
—*Proverbs 31:12*

I seek wool, and flax, and I work willingly with my hands.
—*Proverbs 31:13*

I am like the merchants' ships; I bring my food from afar.
—*Proverbs 31:14*

I rise also while it is yet night, and I give meat to
my household, and a portion to my maidens.
—*Proverbs 31:15*

I consider a field, and buy it: with the fruit
of my hands I plant a vineyard.
—*Proverbs 31:16*

I gird my loins with strength, and strengthen my arms.
—*Proverbs 31:17*

I perceive that my merchandise is good:
my candle goes not out by night.
—*Proverbs 31:18*

I lay my hands to the spindle, and my hands hold the distaff.
—*Proverbs 31:19*

I stretch out my hand to the poor; yea, I
reach forth my hands to the needy.
—*Proverbs 31:20*

I am not afraid of the snow for my household: for
all my household are clothed with scarlet.
—*Proverbs 31:21*

I make myself coverings of tapestry;
my clothing is silk and purple.
—*Proverbs 31:22*

My husband is known in the gates, when he
sits among the elders of the land.
—*Proverbs 31:23*

I make fine linen, and sell it; and I deliver
girdles unto the merchant.
—*Proverbs 31:24*

Strength and honour are my clothing; and I rejoice in time to come.
—*Proverbs 31:25*

I open my mouth with wisdom; and in my
tongue is the law of kindness.
—*Proverbs 31:26*

I look well to the ways of my household,
and I eat not the bread of idleness.
—*Proverbs 31:27*

My children arise up, and call me blessed;
my husband also, and he praises me.
—*Proverbs 31:28*

Many daughters have done virtuously, but I excellest them all.
—*Proverbs 31:29*

Favour is deceitful, and beauty is vain: but a woman
that fears you, O Lord, she shall be praised.
—*Proverbs 31:30*

Give me of the fruit of my hands, O Lord; and
let my own works praise me in the gates.
—*Proverbs 31:31*

O Lord, you make my husband plenteous in
goods and in the fruit of his body.
—*Deuteronomy 28:11*

Blessed is the fruit of my husband's body
and the fruit of his ground.
—*Deuteronomy 28:4*

My husband is filled with the knowledge of your will,
O Lord, in all wisdom and spiritual understanding.
—*Colossians 1:9*

My husband walks worthy of you, O Lord, unto
all pleasing, being fruitful in every good work,
and increasing in your knowledge, O God.
—*Colossians 1:10*

My husband is strengthened with all might, according to your
glorious power, unto all patience and longsuffering with joyfulness.
—*Colossians 1:11*

My husband is your sheep, Lord Jesus, he hears your
voice, and you know him, and he follows you.
—*John 10:27*

My husband is prosperous in all things and
in health, even as his soul prospers.
—3 John 1:2

O Lord, you perfect that which concerns my
husband, your mercy, O Lord, endures forever.
—Psalm 138:8

My husband is a good gift and perfect gift from above,
which came from you, O Father of lights, with whom
is no variableness, neither shadow of turning.
—James 1:17

My husband is blessed with all spiritual
blessings in heavenly places in Christ.
—Ephesians 1:3

With long life you satisfy my husband, O
Lord, and show him your salvation.
—Psalm 91:16

I reverence my husband.
—Ephesians 5:33

I endeavour to keep the unity of the Spirit in
the bond of peace with my husband.
—Ephesians 4:3

O Lord, you redeem my husband's life from destruction; and
you crown him with lovingkindness and tender mercies.
—Psalm 103:4

My husband is complete in you, O Lord, which
is the head of all principality and power.
—Colossians 2:10

My husband is filled with the fruits of righteousness, which are by Jesus Christ, unto your glory and praise, O God.
—*Philippians 1:11*

Now the God of hope fills my husband with all joy and peace in believing, that he may abound in hope, through the power of the Holy Ghost.
—*Romans 15:13*

I speak that my husband continues in the faith grounded and settled, and he is not moved away from the hope of the gospel, which he has heard, and which was preached to him.
—*Colossians 1:23*

Lord, you bless my husband, and you keep him.
—*Numbers 6:24*

O Lord, you make your face shine upon my husband, and you are gracious unto him.
—*Numbers 6:25*

Lord, you satisfy my husband's mouth with good things, so that his youth is renewed like the eagle's.
—*Psalm 103:5*

Lord, you lift up your countenance upon my husband, and you give him peace.
—*Numbers 6:26*

O Lord, you give strength unto my husband; Lord, you bless my husband with peace.
—*Psalm 29:11*

~ 20 ~

Husbands' Confessions

Father, you have given me the woman of my dreams, a woman who completes me and adds meaning and joy to my life.

Thank you, Father, for giving me a wife who submits to my authority as head of our family, head of our home, and as covering over her life.

I honor my wife not as weak but as the weaker vessel, which means I cover her with my strength and provide for her needs.

I choose also to submit myself to my wife in the fear of God, and I choose to love her as I love my own body and as you love the church.

So thank you, Father, for covering our marriage in your love, in your strength, and in your peace. Therefore, O Lord,

I so love my wife even as myself.
—*Ephesians 5:33*

I dwell in a peaceable habitation with my wife, and
in sure dwellings, and in quiet resting places.
—*Isaiah 32:18*

I love my wife, even as you, Jesus Christ, also
love the church, and gave yourself for it.
—*Ephesians 5:25*

I love my wife as my own body. Because
I love my wife, I love myself.
—*Ephesians 5:28*

I render unto my wife due benevolence.
—*1 Corinthians 7:3*

I have not power of my own body, but my wife.
—*1 Corinthians 7:4*

My wife and I submit ourselves to one another in the fear of God.
—*Ephesians 5:21*

I defraud not my wife, except it be with consent for a time, that I
may give myself to fasting and prayer; and we come together again.
—*1 Corinthians 7:5*

My wife and I do not render evil for evil, or railing for
railing: but contrariwise blessing; knowing that we are
thereunto called, that we should inherit a blessing.
—*1 Peter 3:9*

My wife walks worthy of you, O Lord, unto all
pleasing, being fruitful in every good work, and
increasing in your knowledge, O God.
—*Colossians 1:10*

My wife is strengthened with all might, according to your glorious
power, unto all patience and longsuffering with joyfulness.
—*Colossians 1:11*

O Lord, you keep my wife in perfect peace, because her
mind is stayed on you, because she trusts in you.
—*Isaiah 26:3*

I dwell with my wife according to knowledge, giving honour
unto her, as unto the weaker vessel, and as being heirs together
of the grace of life; that my prayers be not hindered.
—*1 Peter 3:7*

My wife and I are of one mind, we have compassion one of
another, we love as brethren, we are pitiful, we are courteous.
—*1 Peter 3:8*

My wife is complete in you, O Lord, which is
the head of all principality and power.
—*Colossians 2:10*

Now the God of hope fills my wife with all joy
and peace in believing, that she may abound in
hope, through the power of the Holy Ghost.
—*Romans 15:13*

My wife is strong in you, O Lord, and in the power of your might.
—*Ephesians 6:10*

O Lord, you give strength unto my wife;
Lord, you bless my wife with peace.
—*Psalm 29:11*

My wife is filled with the knowledge of your will, O
Lord, in all wisdom and spiritual understanding.
—*Colossians 1:9*

I speak that my wife continues in the faith grounded and
settled, and she is not moved away from the hope of the gospel,
which she has heard, and which was preached to her.
—*Colossians 1:23*

My wife is blessed with all spiritual blessings
in heavenly places in Christ.
—*Ephesians 1:3*

My wife is prosperous in all things and in
health, even as her soul prospers.
—*3 John 1:2*

I endeavour to keep the unity of the Spirit
in the bond of peace with my wife.
—*Ephesians 4:3*

I leave my father and mother, and I am joined
unto my wife, and we two are one flesh.
—*Ephesians 5:31*

I live joyfully with my wife whom I love all the days of my life.
—*Ecclesiastes 9:9*

Blessed are you, O Lord, who daily loads my wife
with benefits, even the God of her salvation.
—*Psalm 68:19*

My wife is a good gift and a perfect gift from above,
which came from you, O Father of lights, with whom
is no variableness, neither shadow of turning.
—*James 1:17*

My fountain is blessed; and I rejoice with the wife of my youth.
—*Proverbs 5:18*

My wife is as the loving hind and pleasant roe; her breast satisfies
me at all times; and I am ravished always with her love.
—*Proverbs 5:19*

I am not ravished with a strange woman, and I
do not embrace the bosom of a stranger.
—Proverbs 5:20

For my ways are before your eyes, O Lord,
and I ponder all my goings.
—Proverbs 5:21

O Lord, the commandment is a lamp; and the law is
light; and reproofs of instruction are the way of life:
—Proverbs 6:23

To keep me from the evil woman, from the
flattery of the tongue of a strange woman.
—Proverbs 6:24

I lust not after her beauty in my heart; neither
do I let her take me with her eyelids.
—Proverbs 6:25

I love my wife, and I am not bitter against her.
—Colossians 3:19

Blessed is the fruit of my wife's body and the fruit of her ground.
—Deuteronomy 28:4

Lord, you redeem my wife's life from destruction; and you
crown her with lovingkindness and tender mercies.
—Psalm 103:4

Lord, you satisfy my wife's mouth with good things,
so that her youth is renewed like the eagle's.
—Psalm 103:5

With long life you satisfy my wife, O Lord,
and show her your salvation.
—*Psalm 91:16*

O Lord, you perfect that which concerns my wife,
your mercy, O Lord, endures forever.
—*Psalm 138:8*

My wife is your sheep, Lord Jesus, she hears your
voice, and you know her, and she follows you.
—*John 10:27*

O Lord, you make my wife plenteous in
goods and in the fruit of her body.
—*Deuteronomy 28:11*

My wife is filled with the fruits of righteousness, which
are by Jesus Christ, unto your glory and praise, O God.
—*Philippians 1:11*

O Lord, you bless my wife, and you keep her.
—*Numbers 6:24*

Lord, you make your face shine upon my
wife, and you are gracious unto her.
—*Numbers 6:25*

O Lord, you lift up your countenance upon
my wife, and you give her peace.
—*Numbers 6:26*

~ 21 ~

Parents' Confessions

Father, I thank you for the role you have provided to me as a parent, to raise my children in a Christian atmosphere. Thank you that my children are precious in your sight and they are precious to me.

I value their very existence, and they add so much love and joy to our family. Help me, Father, to continue to raise them in the nurture and admonition of you, O Lord.

I realize that if I love my children, I will also discipline them in love— your love, O God. I speak your blessings over them that they will fulfill your purpose for their lives in this earth, that they will walk and live in health, peace, love, and prosperity all the days of their lives.

I thank you that you satisfy my children with long life and you show them your salvation because they honor you, O Lord, and because they honor their parents. Therefore,

I train up my child in the way he should go: and
when he is old, he will not depart from it.
—Proverbs 22:6

I rule well my own house, having my children
in subjection with all gravity.
—1 Timothy 3:4

I provoke not my children to anger, lest they be discouraged.
—Colossians 3:21

I provoke not my children to wrath: but I bring them
up in the nurture and admonition of you, O Lord.
—*Ephesians 6:4*

I provide for my own, and specially for those of my own house.
—*1 Timothy 5:8*

I have no greater joy than to hear that my children walk in truth.
—*3 John 1:4*

My children are blessed with all spiritual
blessings in heavenly places in Christ.
—*Ephesians 1:3*

My children are filled with the knowledge of your will,
O Lord, in all wisdom and spiritual understanding.
—*Colossians 1:9*

My children are strong in you, O Lord,
and in the power of your might.
—*Ephesians 6:10*

My children are complete in you, O Lord, which
is the head of all principality and power.
—*Colossians 2:10*

My children dwell in the secret place of the most High
and they abide under the shadow of the Almighty.
—*Psalm 91:1*

I will say of you, O Lord, you are my children's refuge
and their fortress: their God; in you they trust.
—*Psalm 91:2*

Surely you deliver my children from the snare of the
fowler, O Lord, and from the noisome pestilence.
—Psalm 91:3

O Lord, you cover my children with your feathers, and under
your wings they trust: your truth is their shield and buckler.
—Psalm 91:4

My children are not afraid for the terror by
night; nor for the arrow that flies by day.
—Psalm 91:5

My children are not afraid for the pestilence that walks in
darkness; nor for the destruction that wastes at noonday.
—Psalm 91:6

A thousand shall fall at my children's side, and ten thousand
at their right hand; but it shall not come nigh them.
—Psalm 91:7

Only with their eyes shall they behold and
see the reward of the wicked.
—Psalm 91:8

My children have made you, O Lord, which is their
refuge, even the most High, their habitation.
—Psalm 91:9

There shall no evil befall my children, neither
shall any plague come nigh their dwelling.
—Psalm 91:10

For you, O Lord, give your angels charge over my
children, to keep them in all their ways.
—Psalm 91:11

Your angels bear my children up in their hands,
lest they dash their foot against a stone.
—*Psalm 91:12*

My children shall tread upon the lion and adder: the young
lion and the dragon shall they trample under feet.
—*Psalm 91:13*

Because my children have set their love upon you,
O Lord, therefore you deliver them: you set them
on high, because they know your name.
—*Psalm 91:14*

My children call upon you, O Lord, and you answer them: you
are with them in trouble; you deliver them, and honour them.
—*Psalm 91:15*

With long life you satisfy my children,
and show them your salvation.
—*Psalm 91:16*

Now the God of hope fills my children with all joy
and peace in believing, that they may abound in
hope, through the power of the Holy Ghost.
—*Romans 15:13*

O Lord, you keep my children in perfect peace, whose
minds are stayed on you, because they trust in you.
—*Isaiah 26:3*

O Lord, you redeem my children's lives from destruction; and
you crown them with lovingkindness and tender mercies.
—*Psalm 103:4*

Lord, you satisfy my children's mouths with good things,
so that their youth is renewed like the eagle's.
—Psalm 103:5

O Lord, you perfect that which concerns my
children, your mercy, O Lord, endures forever.
—Psalm 138:8

All my children are taught of you, O Lord;
and great is the peace of my children.
—Isaiah 54:13

I teach your words to my children, speaking of
them when I sit in my house, and when I walk by
the way, when I lie down, and when I rise up.
—Deuteronomy 11:19

I am a good man and I leave an inheritance to my children's
children: and the wealth of the sinner is laid up for them.
—Proverbs 13:22

My children are a good gift and perfect gift from above,
which came from you, O Father of lights, with whom
is no variableness, neither shadow of turning.
—James 1:17

I despise not my children; for in heaven their angels do
always behold the face of my Father which is in heaven.
—Matthew 18:10

My children receive the blessing from you, O Lord,
and righteousness from the God of their salvation.
—Psalm 24:5

I suffer my little children to come unto you, Lord Jesus, and
I forbid them not: for of such is the kingdom of God.
—Mark 10:14

I spare not my rod because I love my children
and I chasten them betimes.
—Proverbs 13:24

I rejoice greatly that I find of my children walking in truth,
as we have received commandment from you, Father.
—2 John 1:4

My children are your sheep, Lord Jesus, they hear your
voice, and you know them, and they follow you.
—John 10:27

My children are strengthened with all might, according to your
glorious power, unto all patience and longsuffering with joyfulness.
—Colossians 1:11

O Lord, you give strength unto my children;
Lord, you bless my children with peace.
—Psalm 29:11

My children walk worthy of you, O Lord, unto
all pleasing, being fruitful in every good work,
and increasing in your knowledge, O God.
—Colossians 1:10

I speak that my children continue in the faith grounded and
settled, and they are not moved away from the hope of the gospel,
which they have heard, and which was preached to them.
—Colossians 1:23

My children are filled with the fruits of righteousness, which
are by Jesus Christ, unto your glory and praise, O God.
—Philippians 1:11

O Lord, you bless my children, and you keep them.
—Numbers 6:24

Lord, you make your face shine upon my
children, and you are gracious unto them.
—Numbers 6:25

O Lord, you lift up your countenance upon my
children, and you give them peace.
—Numbers 6:26

~ 22 ~

Children's Confessions

Father, I thank you that you have blessed me with godly parents who pray for me daily and watch over my soul. I thank you that my parents are helping me to grow into the mature and responsible person that you desire for me to be.

Thank you for blessing my parents so that they can provide for my every need, and I appreciate all you have enabled them to do for me.

Father, I honor my parents so that my days will be long on this earth and so that I may fulfill the purpose that you have predestined for me before the foundations of the world.

I choose to honor your word, obey my parents' rules, and walk in love with my family and friends. Therefore,

I honour my father and mother; which is the
first commandment with promise.
—Ephesians 6:2

I honour my father and my mother: that my days may be
long upon the land which you, O Lord my God, give me.
—Exodus 20:12

I honour my father and my mother, as you, O Lord my God, has
commanded me; that my days may be prolonged, and that it may
go well with me, in the land which the Lord my God gives me.
—Deuteronomy 5:16

I obey my parents in all things: for this is
well pleasing unto you, O Lord.
—Colossians 3:20

I love not the world, neither the things that are in the world.
—1 John 2:15

I confess my sins, O God, you are faithful and just to forgive
me my sins, and to cleanse me from all unrighteousness.
—1 John 1:9

I obey my parents in the Lord, for this is right.
—Ephesians 6:1

I flee fornication, so that I do not sin against my own body.
—1 Corinthians 6:18

I keep myself from idols. Amen.
—1 John 5:21

I let nothing be done through strife or vainglory; but in
lowliness of mind I esteem others better than myself.
—Philippians 2:3

For this is your will, O God, even my sanctification,
that I abstain from fornication.
—1 Thessalonians 4:3

I repent therefore, and I am converted, that my sins
may be blotted out, when the times of refreshing
shall come from your presence, O Lord.
—Acts 3:19

O Lord, I give you my heart, and I let my eyes observe your ways.
—Proverbs 23:26

I hear the instruction of my father, and I
forsake not the law of my mother.
—Proverbs 1:8

I walk in the light, as you, O God, are in the light, I
have fellowship with others, and the blood of Jesus
Christ your Son cleanses me from all sin.
—1 John 1:7

I know the truth, and the truth makes me free.
—John 8:32

Wherefore seeing I also am compassed about with so
great a cloud of witnesses, I lay aside every weight,
and the sin which does so easily beset me, and I run
with patience the race that is set before me.
—Hebrews 12:1

I let not my adorning be that outward adorning of plaiting my
hair, and of wearing of gold, or of putting on of apparel.
—1 Peter 3:3

But I let my adorning be the hidden man of my heart, in that
which is not corruptible, even the ornament of a meek and
quiet spirit, which is in your sight, O God, of great price.
—1 Peter 3:4

As newborn babes, I desire the sincere milk
of the word, that I may grow thereby.
—1 Peter 2:2

As obedient children, I do not fashion myself
according to the former lusts in my ignorance.
—1 Peter 1:14

I purge myself from dishonourable things, I am a vessel
unto honour, sanctified, and meet for the master's
use, and prepared unto every good work.
—2 Timothy 2:21

I flee also youthful lusts: but I follow righteousness, faith, charity,
peace, with them that call on you, O Lord, out of a pure heart.
—2 Timothy 2:22

Lord, you keep me in perfect peace, because my
mind is stayed on you: because I trust in you.
—Isaiah 26:3

I can do all things through Christ which strengthens me.
—Philippians 4:13

I let no man despise my youth; but I am an
example of the believers, in word, in conversation,
in charity, in spirit, in faith, in purity.
—1 Timothy 4:12

I give attendance to reading, to exhortation, to doctrine.
—1 Timothy 4:13

I am careful for nothing; but in everything by
prayer and supplication with thanksgiving I let my
requests be made known unto you, O God.
—Philippians 4:6

And your peace, O God, which passes all understanding,
keeps my heart and mind through Christ Jesus.
—Philippians 4:7

Finally, whatsoever things are true, whatsoever things are honest, whatsoever things are just, whatsoever things are pure, whatsoever things are lovely, whatsoever things are of good report; if there be any virtue, and if there be any praise, I think on these things.
—*Philippians 4:8*

I both lay me down in peace, and sleep: for you, O Lord, only make me dwell in safety.
—*Psalm 4:8*

When I lie down, I shall not be afraid: yea, I shall lie down, and my sleep shall be sweet.
—*Proverbs 3:24*

My faith comes by hearing, and hearing by your word, O God.
—*Romans 10:17*

What things soever I desire, when I pray, I believe that I receive them, and I have them.
—*Mark 11:24*

I have faith in you, O God.
—*Mark 11:22*

I trust in you, O Lord, with all my heart; and I lean not unto my own understanding.
—*Proverbs 3:5*

In all my ways I acknowledge you, O Lord, and you direct my paths.
—*Proverbs 3:6*

I call those things which be not as though they were.
—*Romans 4:17*

While I look not at the things which are seen, but at the things which are not seen: for the things which are seen are temporal; but the things which are not seen are eternal.
—*2 Corinthians 4:18*

I walk by faith, not by sight.
—*2 Corinthians 5:7*

I am the righteousness of God in Christ Jesus because you, Lord Jesus, who knew no sin became sin for me.
—*2 Corinthians 5:21*

I hunger and thirst after righteousness: for I am filled.
—*Matthew 5:6*

I am more than a conqueror through you,
Christ Jesus, that loved me.
—*Romans 8:37*

I yield my members a servant to righteousness unto holiness.
—*Romans 6:19*

I am crucified with Christ: nevertheless I live; yet not I, but Christ lives in me: and the life which I now live in the flesh I live by the faith of the Son of God, who loved me, and gave himself for me.
—*Galatians 2:20*

I am in Christ, I am a new creature: old things are passed away; behold, all things are become new.
—*2 Corinthians 5:17*

I am complete in you, O Lord, which is the head of all principality and power.
—*Colossians 2:10*

I am your child, O God, by faith in Christ Jesus.
—*Galatians 3:26*

I am strong in you, O Lord, and in the power of your might.
—*Ephesians 6:10*

I am the temple of God, and your Spirit, O God, dwells in me.
—*1 Corinthians 3:16*

I let patience have her perfect work, that I may
be perfect and entire, wanting nothing.
—*James 1:4*

I am prosperous in all things and in health,
even as my soul prospers.
—*3 John 1:2*

There shall no evil befall me, neither shall
any plague come nigh my dwelling.
—*Psalm 91:10*

For you give your angels charge over me,
to keep me in all my ways.
—*Psalm 91:11*

I am blessed in the city, and I am blessed in the field.
—*Deuteronomy 28:3*

You, O God, supply all my need according to
your riches in glory by Christ Jesus.
—*Philippians 4:19*

I delight myself also in you, O Lord, and you
give me the desires of my heart.
—*Psalm 37:4*

And this is the confidence that I have in you, O Lord, that,
if I ask any thing according to your will, you hear me.
—1 John 5:14

And if I know that you hear me, whatsoever I ask, I
know that I have the petitions that I desired of you.
—1 John 5:15

I am swift to hear, I am slow to speak, I am slow to wrath.
—James 1:19

I let this mind be in me, which was also in you, Christ Jesus.
—Philippians 2:5

I cast down imaginations, and every high thing that exalts
itself against the knowledge of God, and I bring into
captivity every thought to the obedience of Christ.
—2 Corinthians 10:5

For you, O God, have not given me the spirit of fear;
but of power, and of love, and of a sound mind.
—2 Timothy 1:7

O Lord, you perfect that which concerns me,
your mercy, O Lord, endures forever.
—Psalm 138:8

There is no fear in my love; but perfect love casts out fear.
—1 John 4:18

I love you, O God, because you first loved me.
—1 John 4:19

I abstain from all appearance of evil.
—*1 Thessalonians 5:22*

I am kind to others, tenderhearted, forgiving others, even
as you, O God, for Christ's sake have forgiven me.
—*Ephesians 4:32*

I continue in the faith grounded and settled, and I am
not moved away from the hope of the gospel, which
I have heard, and which was preached to me.
—*Colossians 1:23*

I am filled with the fruits of righteousness, which are by
Jesus Christ, unto your glory and praise, O God.
—*Philippians 1:11*

I stagger not at your promise, O God, through unbelief;
but I am strong in faith, I give glory to God.
—*Romans 4:20*

I am fully persuaded that, what you have promised,
O God, you are able also to perform.
—*Romans 4:21*

I am confident of this very thing, that you, O
Lord, who have begun a good work in me will
perform it until the day of Jesus Christ.
—*Philippians 1:6*

~ 23 ~

Prayer for Pastors

Father, thank you for giving us pastors after your own heart. You have called and anointed them to shepherd your flock in the earth.

You have chosen them to help guide us to knowledge and wisdom of your word and to lead us to a rich and meaningful relationship with you.

I thank you, Father, for daily supplying their every need and continually speaking to their hearts fresh manna and revelation to impart to your people.

Father, I pray you let them preach your word with clarity, that they speak as the oracles of God, and let them minister with the ability that you give in love.

Father, I pray that they operate with holy boldness and that you continue to open unto them a door of utterance that they will speak your mysteries. Therefore,

Thank you, Father, for giving us pastors according to your
heart, which feed us with knowledge and understanding.
—*Jeremiah 3:15*

Father, let my pastors speak as the oracles of God; let them
minister as of the ability which you give, O God: that you
in all things may be glorified through Jesus Christ, to
whom be praise and dominion for ever and ever. Amen.
—*1 Peter 4:11*

Father, let my pastors preach the word; let them be
instant in season, out of season; let them reprove,
rebuke, exhort with all longsuffering and doctrine.
—*2 Timothy 4:2*

I pray that utterance may be given unto my pastors, that they may
open their mouth boldly, to make known the mystery of the gospel.
—*Ephesians 6:19*

I pray my pastors be strong in the grace that is in Christ Jesus.
—*2 Timothy 2:1*

Father, I pray that you open unto my pastors a door
of utterance, to speak the mystery of Christ.
—*Colossians 4:3*

I pray that my pastors may make it
manifest, as they ought to speak.
—*Colossians 4:4*

Father, I pray that my pastors walk in wisdom toward
them that are without, redeeming the time.
—*Colossians 4:5*

I pray that my pastor's speech be always with grace, seasoned with
salt, that they may know how they ought to answer every man.
—*Colossians 4:6*

Father, I speak that my pastor's speech and their
preaching is not with enticing words of man's wisdom,
but in demonstration of the Spirit and of power.
—*1 Corinthians 2:4*

I speak that my pastor's faith does not stand in the
wisdom of men, but in your power, O God.
—*1 Corinthians 2:5*

Thank you, Father, that my pastors speak your wisdom
in a mystery, even the hidden wisdom, which you
ordained before the world unto our glory.
—1 Corinthians 2:7

Thank you, Father, that you are of power to stablish my
pastors according to your gospel, and the preaching of
Jesus Christ, according to the revelation of the mystery,
which was kept secret since the world began.
—Romans 16:25

Thank you, Lord God, that you have given my pastors the
tongue of the learned, that they should know how to speak
a word in season to him who is weary: you wake morning
by morning, you wake their ears to hear as the learned.
—Isaiah 50:4

Thank you, Father, that my pastors are ambassadors in bonds:
that therein they speak boldly, as they ought to speak.
—Ephesians 6:20

Your Spirit, O Lord, is upon my pastors, because you
have anointed them to preach the gospel to the poor;
you have sent them to heal the brokenhearted, to preach
deliverance to the captives, and recovering of sight to
the blind, to set at liberty them that are bruised.
—Luke 4:18

You have anointed my pastors to preach
your acceptable year, O Lord.
—Luke 4:19

My pastors are your sheep, Lord Jesus, they hear your
voice, and you know them, and they follow you.
—John 10:27

For the Lord Jesus Christ's sake, and for the love
of the Spirit, I strive together with my pastors
in my prayers to you, O God, for them.
—*Romans 15:30*

Father, I pray that my pastors may be delivered from them
that do not believe in Judea; and that their service which
they have for Jerusalem may be accepted of the saints.
—*Romans 15:31*

Father, I pray that my pastors may come to me with joy
by your will, O God, and may with me be refreshed.
—*Romans 15:32*

Thank you, Father, that my pastors are full of goodness, they are
filled with all knowledge, and they are able to admonish others.
—*Romans 15:14*

O God, you make all grace abound toward my
pastors; that they, always having all sufficiency in
all things, may abound to every good work.
—*2 Corinthians 9:8*

I pray that you, O God of my Lord Jesus Christ, the
Father of glory, may give unto my pastors the spirit of
wisdom and revelation in the knowledge of him.
—*Ephesians 1:17*

Father, I pray that the eyes of my pastor's understanding
are enlightened; that they may know what is the
hope of your calling, and what the riches of the
glory of your inheritance in the saints.
—*Ephesians 1:18*

Father, I pray that my pastors know what is the exceeding
greatness of your power to us-ward who believe,
according to the working of your mighty power.
—*Ephesians 1:19*

O Lord, I pray that my pastors abound in every
thing, in faith, and utterance, and knowledge, and
in all diligence, and in your love to us.
—*2 Corinthians 8:7*

Holy Spirit, you are the Spirit of truth, you have
come, you guide my pastors into all truth: for you do
not speak of yourself; but whatsoever you hear, that
you speak: and you show them things to come.
—*John 16:13*

Thank you, Father, that in every thing my pastors are
enriched by you, in all utterance, and in all knowledge.
—*1 Corinthians 1:5*

Father, I pray that my pastors come behind in no gift;
waiting for the coming of our Lord Jesus Christ.
—*1 Corinthians 1:7*

I do not cease to pray for my pastors, and to desire that
they might be filled with the knowledge of your will, O
Lord, in all wisdom and spiritual understanding.
—*Colossians 1:9*

Father, I pray that my pastors might walk worthy of you,
O Lord, unto all pleasing, being fruitful in every good
work, and increasing in your knowledge, O God.
—*Colossians 1:10*

Father, I pray that my pastors are strengthened with
all might, according to your glorious power, unto all
patience and longsuffering with joyfulness.
—*Colossians 1:11*

I pray that my pastors continue in the faith grounded and
settled, and are not moved away from the hope of the gospel.
—*Colossians 1:23*

Father, I pray for my pastors, that your word, O Lord, may
have free course, and be glorified, even as it is with you.
—*2 Thessalonians 3:1*

Father, I pray that your love may abound in my pastors
yet more and more in knowledge and in all judgment.
—*Philippians 1:9*

O Lord, you perfect that which concerns my pastors,
your mercy, O Lord, endures forever.
—*Psalm 138:8*

Father, I pray that my pastors may approve things that are excellent;
that they may be sincere and without offence till the day of Christ.
—*Philippians 1:10*

Thank you, Father, that my pastors are filled with
the fruits of righteousness, which are by Jesus
Christ, unto your glory and praise, O God.
—*Philippians 1:11*

Father, I pray that my pastors are delivered from the
snare of the fowler, and from the noisome pestilence.
—*Psalm 91:3*

Thank you, God, for covering my pastors with your feathers, and under your wings they trust: your truth is their shield and bucker.
—Psalm 91:4

Father, thank you that a thousand shall fall at my pastor's side, and ten thousand at their right hand; but it shall not come nigh them.
—Psalm 91:7

Thank you, Father, that my pastors put the brethren
in remembrance of these things, they are your good
ministers, Jesus Christ, nourished up in the words of faith
and of good doctrine, whereunto they have attained.
—1 Timothy 4:6

Thank you, Father, that my pastors are your
servants, O Lord, and they do not strive; but they
are gentle unto all men, apt to teach, patient.
—2 Timothy 2:24

Father, I thank you that my pastors grow in grace, and in
the knowledge of our Lord and Saviour Jesus Christ.
—2 Peter 3:18

~ 24 ~

Prayer for the Church
(Corporate Confessions)

Thank you, Father, for giving us a church built by your word and designed for your purpose in this community and in this world. We thank you for making our church strong in you, O Lord, and in the power of your might.

Thank you that your love abides in our church and your love seals our church in the unity of your Spirit. Thank you, Father, for adding to our number daily, such as should be saved.

Though we are many members, we are one body—the body of Christ—and we are members one of another. Father, thank you for giving us access into your presence as we commune with you in worship and adoration.

Father, let our church be filled with your love so that your glory will fill our temple and that our offerings will be a sweet-smelling sacrifice unto you. Therefore,

We confess that our church fulfils your joy, that we are likeminded, we have the same love, we are of one accord, we have one mind.
—*Philippians 2:2*

We let nothing be done through strife or vainglory; but in lowliness of mind we each esteem others better than ourselves.
—*Philippians 2:3*

Thank you, Father, that our church is established in
the faith, and we increase in number daily.
—*Acts 16:5*

Unto you, O God, be glory in our church by Christ Jesus
throughout all ages, world without end. Amen.
—*Ephesians 3:21*

O God, you are faithful, by you we were called unto
the fellowship of your Son Jesus Christ our Lord.
—*1 Corinthians 1:9*

Our church receives power, for the Holy Ghost is come upon us;
and we are witnesses unto you, O Lord, both in Jerusalem, and in
all Judaea, and in Samaria, and unto the uttermost part of the earth.
—*Acts 1:8*

Lord Jesus, you are the Christ, the Son of the living God.
—*Matthew 16:16*

And upon this rock you build your church; and
the gates of hell shall not prevail against it.
—*Matthew 16:18*

Thank you Lord for adding to our church
daily such as should be saved.
—*Acts 2:47*

We are labourers together with you, O God: we
are your husbandry, we are your building.
—*1 Corinthians 3:9*

Our church is built upon the foundation of the apostles and
prophets, Jesus Christ himself being the chief corner stone.
—*Ephesians 2:20*

In you all the building fitly framed together grows
unto an holy temple in you, O Lord.
—*Ephesians 2:21*

In you, Lord Jesus, we also are built together for
an habitation of God through the Spirit.
—*Ephesians 2:22*

Father, we pray that our hearts might be comforted,
being knit together in love, and unto all riches of the full
assurance of understanding, to the acknowledgement of
your mystery, O God, and of the Father, and of Christ.
—*Colossians 2:2*

Lord Jesus, you are the head of the body, the church:
you are the beginning, the firstborn from the dead; that
in all things you might have the preeminence.
—*Colossians 1:18*

Father, we pray that our church continues in the faith grounded
and settled, and that we are not moved away from the hope of the
gospel, which we have heard, and which was preached to us.
—*Colossians 1:23*

Thank you, Father, that our church continues
steadfastly in the apostles' doctrine and fellowship,
and in breaking of bread, and in prayers.
—*Acts 2:42*

As your church, Lord Jesus, we only let our conversation be as
it becomes the gospel of Christ: and we stand fast in one spirit,
with one mind striving together for the faith of the gospel.
—*Philippians 1:27*

Thank you, Father, that the mystery which has been hid from
ages and from generations, is now made manifest to your saints.
—Colossians 1:26

We walk in the light, as you, O God, are in the light,
we have fellowship one with another, and the blood of
Jesus Christ your Son cleanses us from all sin.
—1 John 1:7

So we, being many, are one body in Christ, and
every one members one of another.
—Romans 12:5

Now you, O God of patience and consolation grant us to be
likeminded one toward another according to Christ Jesus:
—Romans 15:5

That we may with one mind and one mouth glorify you,
O God, even the Father of our Lord Jesus Christ.
—Romans 15:6

Wherefore receive we one another, as Christ
also received us to your glory, O God.
—Romans 15:7

Father, we pray that your love may abound in our church
yet more and more in knowledge and in all judgment.
—Philippians 1:9

Father, we pray that our church may approve
things that are excellent; that we may be sincere
and without offence till the day of Christ.
—Philippians 1:10

Thank you, Father, that our church is filled with
the fruits of righteousness, which are by Jesus
Christ, unto your glory and praise, O God.
—*Philippians 1:11*

We walk honestly, as in the day; not in rioting and drunkenness,
not in chambering and wantonness, not in strife and envying.
—*Romans 13:13*

As we have therefore opportunity, we do good unto all men,
especially unto them who are of the household of faith.
—*Galatians 6:10*

We walk worthy of the vocation wherewith we are called.
—*Ephesians 4:1*

With all lowliness and meekness, with longsuffering,
we forbear one another in love.
—*Ephesians 4:2*

We endeavour to keep the unity of the Spirit in the bond of peace.
—*Ephesians 4:3*

There is one body, and one Spirit, even as we are
called in one hope of your calling, O Lord.
—*Ephesians 4:4*

Thank you, Father, that to our church, you gave
some, apostles; and some, prophets; and some,
evangelists; and some, pastors and teachers;
—*Ephesians 4:11*

For the perfecting of the saints, for the work of the
ministry, for the edifying of the body of Christ:
—*Ephesians 4:12*

Till we all come in the unity of the faith, and of the
knowledge of the Son of God, unto a perfect man, unto
the measure of the stature of the fulness of Christ:
—*Ephesians 4:13*

That we henceforth be no more children, tossed to and fro, and
carried about with every wind of doctrine, by the sleight of men,
and cunning craftiness, whereby they lie in wait to deceive;
—*Ephesians 4:14*

But we speak the truth in love, that we may grow up into
you in all things, which is the head, even Christ:
—*Ephesians 4:15*

From whom our whole body fitly jointed together and
compacted by that which every joint supplies, according to
the effectual working in the measure of every part, makes
increase of the body unto the edifying of itself in love.
—*Ephesians 4:16*

We henceforth walk not as other Gentiles
walk, in the vanity of their mind.
—*Ephesians 4:17*

We put off concerning the former conversation the old
man, which is corrupt according to the deceitful lusts.
—*Ephesians 4:22*

We are renewed in the spirit of our minds.
—*Ephesians 4:23*

We put on the new man, which after you, O God,
is created in righteousness and true holiness.
—*Ephesians 4:24*

Wherefore we put away lying, we speak every man truth
with our neighbor: for we are members one of another.
—*Ephesians 4:25*

Be ye angry, and sin not: we let not the
sun go down upon our wrath.
—*Ephesians 4:26*

Neither give we place to the devil.
—*Ephesians 4:27*

If we have stolen, we steal no more: but rather we
labour, working with our hands the thing which is
good, that we may have to give to him that need.
—*Ephesians 4:28*

We let no corrupt communication proceed out of our
mouths, but that which is good to the use of edifying,
that it may minister grace unto the hearers.
—*Ephesians 4:29*

We grieve not the holy Spirit of God, whereby
we are sealed unto the day of redemption.
—*Ephesians 4:30*

We let all bitterness, and wrath, and anger, and clamour,
and evil speaking, be put away from us, with all malice.
—*Ephesians 4:31*

We are kind one to another, tenderhearted, forgiving one another,
even as you, O God, for Christ's sake have forgiven us.
—*Ephesians 4:32*

We all are of one mind, we have compassion one of another,
we love as brethren, we are pitiful, we are courteous.
—*1 Peter 3:8*

We do not render evil for evil, or railing for railing: but contrariwise blessing; knowing that we are thereunto called, that we should inherit a blessing.
—1 Peter 3:9

We purge ourselves from dishonourable things, we are vessels unto honour, sanctified, and meet for the master's use, and prepared unto every good work.
—2 Timothy 2:21

We flee also youthful lusts: but we follow righteousness, faith, charity, peace, with them that call on you, O Lord, out of a pure heart.
—2 Timothy 2:22

Father, we draw near with a true heart in full assurance of faith, having our hearts sprinkled from an evil conscience, and our bodies washed with pure water.
—Hebrews 10:22

We hold fast the profession of our faith without wavering; for you, O Lord, are faithful that promised.
—Hebrews 10:23

And we consider one another to provoke unto love and to good works.
—Hebrews 10:24

We forsake not the assembling of ourselves together, as the manner of some is; but we exhort one another: and so much the more, as we see the day approaching.
—Hebrews 10:25

We having the same spirit of faith, according as it
is written, I believed, and therefore have I spoken;
we also believe, and therefore speak.
—2 Corinthians 4:13

We know that you, O God, which raised up the Lord Jesus
shall raise up us also by Jesus, and shall present us with you.
—2 Corinthians 4:14

For which cause we faint not; but though our outward man
perish, yet the inward man is renewed day by day.
—2 Corinthians 4:16

For our light affliction, which is but for a moment, works
for us a far more exceeding and eternal weight of glory.
—2 Corinthians 4:17

While we look not at the things which are seen, but at the
things which are not seen: for the things which are seen are
temporal; but the things which are not seen are eternal.
—2 Corinthians 4:18

For by one Spirit are we all baptized into one body,
whether we be Jews or Gentiles, whether we be bond or
free; and have been all made to drink into one Spirit.
—1 Corinthians 12:13

For the body is not one member, but many.
—1 Corinthians 12:14

Forasmuch as we are zealous of spiritual gifts, we seek
that we may excel to the edifying of the church.
—1 Corinthians 14:12

O Lord, you perfect that which concerns our
church, your mercy, O Lord, endures forever.
—Psalm 138:8

For we also, as lively stones, are built up a spiritual
house, an holy priesthood, to offer up spiritual sacrifices,
acceptable to you, O God, by Jesus Christ.
—1 Peter 2:5

By your name, Lord Jesus Christ, we all speak the same thing,
and there are no divisions among us; but we are perfectly
joined together in the same mind and in the same judgment.
—1 Corinthians 1:10

~ 25 ~

Divine Protection

Thank you, Father, that you have promised never to leave me or forsake me. You promised to always be with me wherever I go.

You are my hiding place, my pavilion, my strong tower in the time of trouble. Knowing that I am never alone, I do not have to walk in fear of anything or anyone.

Father, your Spirit lives in me and constantly leads and guides me in all the ways of truth. Therefore,

You, O Lord, are my light and my salvation; whom shall I fear?
You are the strength of my life; of whom shall I be afraid?
—Psalm 27:1

When the wicked, even mine enemies and my foes, came
upon me to eat up my flesh, they stumbled and fell.
—Psalm 27:2

Though a host should encamp against me, my heart shall not fear:
though war should rise against me, in this will I be confident.
—Psalm 27:3

One thing have I desired of you, O Lord, that will I seek after;
that I may dwell in the house of the Lord all the days of my life,
to behold your beauty, O Lord, and to enquire in your temple.
—Psalm 27:4

For in the time of trouble you hide me in your pavilion: in the secret of your tabernacle you hide me; you set me up upon a rock.
—*Psalm 27:5*

You are my hiding place, O Lord; you preserve me from trouble; you compass me about with songs of deliverance.
—*Psalm 32:7*

O Lord, you fight for me, and I hold my peace.
—*Exodus 14:14*

I dwell in the secret place of the most High and I abide under the shadow of the Almighty.
—*Psalm 91:1*

I say of you, O Lord, you are my refuge and my fortress: my God; in you I trust.
—*Psalm 91:2*

You deliver me from the snare of the fowler, O Lord, and from the noisome pestilence.
—*Psalm 91:3*

O Lord, you cover me with your feathers, and under your wings I trust: your truth is my shield and buckler.
—*Psalm 91:4*

I am not afraid for the terror by night; nor for the arrow that flies by day.
—*Psalm 91:5*

I am not afraid for the pestilence that walks in darkness; nor for the destruction that wastes at noonday.
—*Psalm 91:6*

A thousand shall fall at my side, and ten thousand at
my right hand; but it shall not come nigh me.
—*Psalm 91:7*

Only with my eyes shall I behold and see the reward of the wicked.
—*Psalm 91:8*

Because I have made you, O Lord, which is my
refuge, even the most High, my habitation.
—*Psalm 91:9*

There shall no evil befall me, neither shall
any plague come nigh my dwelling.
—*Psalm 91:10*

For you give your angels charge over me,
to keep me in all my ways.
—*Psalm 91:11*

Your angels bear me up in their hands, lest
I dash my foot against a stone.
—*Psalm 91:12*

I tread upon the lion and adder: the young lion
and the dragon I trample under feet.
—*Psalm 91:13*

Because I have set my love upon you, O Lord, therefore, you
deliver me: you set me on high, because I know your name.
—*Psalm 91:14*

I call upon you, O Lord, and you answer me: you are
with me in trouble; you deliver me, and honour me.
—*Psalm 91:15*

With long life you satisfy me, O Lord, and show me your salvation.
—*Psalm 91:16*

Father, you hide me in the secret of your presence from the pride of man: you keep me secretly in a pavilion from the strife of tongues.
—*Psalm 31:20*

You redeem my life from destruction, O Lord; you crown me with lovingkindness and tender mercies.
—*Psalm 103:4*

I am strong and of a good courage, I fear not, nor am I afraid of them: for you, O Lord my God, do go with me; you will not fail me, nor forsake me.
—*Deuteronomy 31:6*

For you, O God, have not given me the spirit of fear; but of power, and of love, and of a sound mind.
—*2 Timothy 1:7*

Your angel, O Lord, encamps round about me because I fear you, and you deliver me.
—*Psalm 34:7*

But you, O Lord, are faithful, you stablish me, and keep me from evil.
—*2 Thessalonians 3:3*

For you, O Lord, are unto me a wall of fire round about, and you are the glory in the midst of me.
—*Zechariah 2:5*

You, O Lord, are a shelter for me, and a strong tower from the enemy.
—*Psalm 61:3*

I am not afraid of ten thousands of people, that
have set themselves against me round about.
—*Psalm 3:6*

In righteousness I am established: I am far from oppression; for
I shall not fear: and from terror; for it shall not come near me.
—*Isaiah 54:14*

When I cry unto you, O Lord, then shall my enemies
turn back: this I know; for you, O God, are for me.
—*Psalm 56:9*

I let my conversation be without covetousness; and
I am content with such things as I have: for you, O
Lord, will never leave me, nor forsake me.
—*Hebrews 13:5*

I boldly say, you, O Lord, are my helper, and I
will not fear what man shall do unto me.
—*Hebrews 13:6*

I cast all my care upon you, O Lord; for you care for me.
—*1 Peter 5:7*

You are for me, O God, who can be against me?
—*Romans 8:31*

I am not afraid of sudden fear, neither of the
desolation of the wicked, when it comes.
—*Proverbs 3:25*

For you, O Lord, are my confidence, and you
keep my foot from being taken.
—*Proverbs 3:26*

O Lord, you bless me, and keep me.
—*Numbers 6:24*

As you have commanded me, O Lord, I am strong and of a good courage; I am not afraid, neither am I dismayed: for you, O Lord my God, are with me whithersoever I go.
—*Joshua 1:9*

Behold, you, O God, are my salvation; I trust, and I am not afraid: for the LORD JEHOVAH is my strength and my song; you also are my salvation.
—*Isaiah 12:2*

~ 26 ~

Victory over the Flesh
(Free from Addictions)

Thank you, Father, for making me victorious in every area of my life through my Lord and Savior, Jesus Christ. Lord Jesus, because of your sacrifice, I am an overcomer.

Your word declares that whatsoever is born of God overcomes the world, and this is the victory that overcomes the world, even my faith.

The world—my flesh or the devil—has no power over me. I am more than a conqueror through Christ Jesus, who loved me. Therefore,

My body is the temple of the Holy Ghost which is in
me, which I have of God, and I am not my own.
—*1 Corinthians 6:19*

For I am bought with a price: therefore I glorify you, O
God, in my body, and in my spirit, which are God's.
—*1 Corinthians 6:20*

Now you, O Lord, are that Spirit: and where
your Spirit is, there is liberty.
—*2 Corinthians 3:17*

I repent therefore, and I am converted, that my sins
may be blotted out, when the times of refreshing
shall come from your presence, O Lord.
—*Acts 3:19*

I deny ungodliness and worldly lusts, I live soberly,
righteously, and godly, in this present world.
—Titus 2:12

I am crucified with Christ: nevertheless I live; yet not I, but Christ
lives in me: and the life which I now live in the flesh I live by the
faith of the Son of God, who loved me, and gave himself for me.
—Galatians 2:20

There has no temptation taken me but such as is common to
man: but you, O God, are faithful, who will not suffer me to
be tempted above that I am able; but will with the temptation
also make a way to escape, that I may be able to bear it.
—1 Corinthians 10:13

For I have not an high priest which cannot be touched
with the feeling of my infirmities; but was in all
points tempted like as I am, yet without sin.
—Hebrews 4:15

I keep my tongue from evil, and my lips from speaking guile.
—Psalm 34:13

O Lord, your grace is sufficient for me: for your
strength is made perfect in weakness.
—2 Corinthians 12:9

I am not drunk with wine, wherein is excess;
but I am filled with the Spirit.
—Ephesians 5:18

All things are lawful unto me, but all things are
not expedient: all things are lawful for me, but I
will not be brought under the power of any.
—1 Corinthians 6:12

The thief comes not, but for to steal, and to kill, and
to destroy: but Lord Jesus, you have come that I might
have life, and that I might have it more abundantly.
—John 10:10

I am buried with you, Lord Jesus, in baptism, wherein
also I am risen with you through the faith of the operation
of God, who has raised you from the dead.
—Colossians 2:12

I flee fornication, so that I do not sin against my own body.
—1 Corinthians 6:18

I keep myself from idols. Amen.
—1 John 5:21

I let nothing be done through strife or vainglory; but in
lowliness of mind I esteem others better than myself.
—Philippians 2:3

I am called unto liberty; I do not use liberty for an
occasion to the flesh, but by love I serve others.
—Galatians 5:13

For this is your will, O God, even my sanctification,
that I abstain from fornication.
—1 Thessalonians 4:3

I stand fast therefore in the liberty wherewith Christ
has made me free, and I am not entangled
again with the yoke of bondage.
—Galatians 5:1

I abstain from all appearance of evil.
—1 Thessalonians 5:22

Wherefore seeing I also am compassed about with so
great a cloud of witnesses, I lay aside every weight,
and the sin which does so easily beset me, and I run
with patience the race that is set before me.
—*Hebrews 12:1*

I confess my sins, O God, you are faithful and just to forgive
me my sins, and to cleanse me from all unrighteousness.
—*1 John 1:9*

I set my affection on things above, not on things on the earth.
—*Colossians 3:2*

I am the temple of God, and your Spirit, O God, dwells in me.
—*1 Corinthians 3:16*

Whereby are given unto me exceeding great and precious
promises: that by these I am a partaker of the divine nature,
having escaped the corruption that is in the world through lusts.
—*2 Peter 1:4*

For you, O God, have not called me unto
uncleanness, but unto holiness.
—*1 Thessalonians 4:7*

I present my body a living sacrifice, holy, acceptable
unto you, O God, which is my reasonable service.
—*Romans 12:1*

I love not the world, neither the things that are in the world.
—*1 John 2:15*

I take no thought for my life, what I shall eat, or what I
shall drink; nor yet for my body, what I shall put on. My
life is more than meat, and my body than raiment.
—*Matthew 6:25*

I am swift to hear, I am slow to speak, I am slow to wrath.
—*James 1:19*

Whether therefore I eat, or drink, or whatsoever
I do, I do all to your glory, O God.
—*1 Corinthians 10:31*

I walk in the light, as you, O God, are in the light, I
have fellowship with others, and the blood of Jesus
Christ your Son cleanses me from all sin.
—*1 John 1:7*

I am not among winebibbers; I am not
among riotous eaters of flesh.
—*Proverbs 23:20*

I am born of you, O God, and I overcome the world: and this
is the victory that overcomes the world, even my faith.
—*1 John 5:4*

The night is far spent, the day is at hand: I therefore cast off
the works of darkness, and I put on the armor of light.
—*Romans 13:12*

I walk honestly, as in the day; not in rioting and drunkenness,
not in chambering and wantonness, not in strife and envying.
—*Romans 13:13*

But I put on the Lord Jesus Christ, and I make not
provision for the flesh, to fulfil the lusts thereof.
—*Romans 13:14*

I take heed lest by any means this liberty of mine
become a stumbling block to them that are weak.
—*1 Corinthians 8:9*

Having therefore these promises, I cleanse
myself from all filthiness of the flesh and spirit,
perfecting holiness in the fear of God.
—*2 Corinthians 7:1*

I mortify my members which are upon the earth;
fornication, uncleanness, inordinate affection, evil
concupiscence, and covetousness, which is idolatry.
—*Colossians 3:5*

As obedient children, I do not fashion myself
according to the former lusts in my ignorance.
—*1 Peter 1:14*

I can do all things through Christ which strengthens me.
—*Philippians 4:13*

I purge myself from dishonourable things, I am a vessel
unto honour, sanctified, and meet for the master's
use, and prepared unto every good work.
—*2 Timothy 2:21*

I flee also youthful lusts: but I follow righteousness, faith, charity,
peace, with them that call on you, O Lord, out of a pure heart.
—*2 Timothy 2:22*

I put off all these; anger, wrath, malice, blasphemy,
filthy communication out of my mouth.
—*Colossians 3:8*

I fear you, O Lord, and I hate evil: pride, and arrogancy,
and the evil way, and the froward mouth, do I hate.
—*Proverbs 8:13*

I am more than a conqueror through you,
Christ Jesus, that loved me.
—*Romans 8:37*

I keep under my body, and I bring it into subjection.
—*1 Corinthians 9:27*

My steps are ordered in your word, O Lord: and
no iniquity have dominion over me.
—*Psalm 119:133*

I am not unequally yoked together with unbelievers: for
what fellowship have righteousness with unrighteousness?
And what communion have light with darkness?
—*2 Corinthians 6:14*

I am the temple of the living God; as you have
said, O God, you dwell in me, and walk in me;
and you are my God, and I am your people.
—*2 Corinthians 6:16*

I am buried with you, Lord Jesus, by baptism into death:
that like as you were raised up from the dead by the glory
of the Father, even so I also walk in newness of life.
—*Romans 6:4*

I am planted together in the likeness of your death, Lord
Jesus, I am also in the likeness of your resurrection.
—*Romans 6:5*

My old man is crucified with you, Lord Jesus,
that the body of sin might be destroyed, that
henceforth I should not serve sin.
—*Romans 6:6*

I reckon also myself dead indeed unto sin, but alive
unto you, O God, through Jesus Christ my Lord.
—*Romans 6:11*

I let not sin therefore reign in my mortal body,
that I should obey it in the lusts thereof.
—*Romans 6:12*

I yield not my members as instruments of unrighteousness unto
sin: but I yield myself unto you, O God, as being alive from the
dead, and my members as instruments of righteousness unto God.
—*Romans 6:13*

Sin does not have dominion over me: for I am
not under the law, but under grace.
—*Romans 6:14*

What then? shall I sin, because I am not under the
law, but under grace? O God, you forbid.
—*Romans 6:15*

I yield myself a servant of obedience unto righteousness.
—*Romans 6:16*

But thank you, O God, that I was the servant of
sin, but I have obeyed from the heart that form
of doctrine which was delivered me.
—*Romans 6:17*

Being then made free from sin, I became
the servant of righteousness.
—*Romans 6:18*

I am not in the flesh, but in the Spirit, for
your Spirit, O God, dwells in me.
—*Romans 8:9*

Christ, you are in me, the body is dead because of sin;
but the Spirit is life because of righteousness.
—*Romans 8:10*

Wherefore I come out from among them, and I am separate, and
I touch not the unclean thing; and you receive me, O Lord.
—*2 Corinthians 6:17*

I touch not; I taste not; I handle not.
—*Colossians 2:21*

I am not deceived: evil communications corrupt good manners.
—*1 Corinthians 15:33*

A stranger will I not follow, but I will flee from
him: for I know not the voice of strangers.
—*John 10:5*

I am made free from sin, and I am your servant, O God, I
have my fruit unto holiness, and the end everlasting life.
—*Romans 6:22*

I come boldly unto your throne of grace, O Lord, that I may
obtain mercy, and find grace to help in time of need.
—*Hebrews 4:16*

I walk in the Spirit, and I do not fulfil the lust of the flesh.
—*Galatians 5:16*

I come after you, Lord Jesus, I deny myself, and
I take up my cross, and I follow you.
—*Matthew 16:24*

The Victor's Confession

Jesus Christ, you have made me free from _____ and I am free indeed! _____ has no control over me. I am free from the strongholds of _____.

My spirit is in control, and my spirit sits on the throne of my heart. My body is the temple of the Holy Ghost, not the temple of _____. I have authority over the suggestion of _____.

My flesh is dead and buried with you, Lord Jesus, in baptism, and _____ does not control my life. I am not weak. I am strong in you, O Lord, and in the power of your might.

I do not comfort my flesh with _____. _____ is not my god, and I do not serve or cater to _____. I do not surrender, submit to, or yield to _____. I am completely submitted to you, O God.

I resist the devil and he flees from me, and I resist _____ and it flees from me. _____ does not have dominion over me.

I am a servant of righteousness. Jesus Christ lives in me. I am more than a conqueror through Christ Jesus.

I can do all things through Christ, who strengthens me. I walk in the spirit and I am called unto liberty. I am free in Jesus's name.

I am free by Jesus's stripes and I walk in newness of life. I walk in the Spirit of the Living God.

Greater is he who is in me than he who is in the world. I am the servant of God Almighty.

In Jesus's name, Amen!

~ 27 ~

Authority and Weaponry

Thank you, Father, that your word encompasses everything I need to defeat all of my enemies, for you have given me authority over them.

I realize that as I submit to you, O God, and live in obedience to your word, the enemy must flee from me when I resist him.

I thank you, Father, for providing your full armor for my protection so that I can fight victoriously. Therefore,

> I am of the day and I am sober, I put on the breastplate of
> faith and love; and for an helmet, the hope of salvation.
> *—1 Thessalonians 5:8*

I build up myself on my most holy faith, praying in the Holy Ghost.
—Jude 1:20

> I submit myself therefore to you, O God. I
> resist the devil, and he flees from me.
> *—James 4:7*

I have power to tread on serpents and scorpions, and over all the
power of the enemy: and nothing shall by any means hurt me.
—Luke 10:19

> O Lord, you cause my enemies that rise up against
> me to be smitten before my face: they shall come out
> against me one way, and flee before me seven ways.
> *—Deuteronomy 28:7*

Lord Jesus, you give unto me the keys of the kingdom of
heaven: and whatsoever I bind on earth is bound in heaven:
and whatsoever I loose on earth is loosed in heaven.
—*Matthew 16:19*

I have power against unclean spirits, to cast them out, and
to heal all manner of sickness and all manner of disease.
—*Matthew 10:1*

Whatsoever I bind on earth is bound in heaven: and
whatsoever I loose on earth is loosed in heaven.
—*Matthew 18:18*

Because I have received you, Lord Jesus,
you gave me power to become the son of God,
because I believe on your name.
—*John 1:12*

I receive power, for the Holy Ghost is come upon me: and I am a
witness unto you, O Lord, both in Jerusalem, and in all Judaea,
and in Samaria, and unto the uttermost part of the earth.
—*Acts 1:8*

I am strong in you, O Lord, and in the power of your might.
—*Ephesians 6:10*

I put on your whole armour, O God, that I may be
able to stand against the wiles of the devil.
—*Ephesians 6:11*

I wrestle not against flesh and blood, but against principalities,
against powers, against the rulers of the darkness of this
world, against spiritual wickedness in high places.
—*Ephesians 6:12*

Wherefore, I take unto me your whole armour, O God, that I may be able to withstand in the evil day, and having done all, to stand.
—*Ephesians 6:13*

I stand therefore, having my loins girt about with truth, and having on the breastplate of righteousness.
—*Ephesians 6:14*

My feet are shod with the preparation of the gospel of peace.
—*Ephesians 6:15*

I take the shield of faith, wherewith I am able to quench all the fiery darts of the wicked.
—*Ephesians 6:16*

I take the helmet of salvation, and the sword of the Spirit, which is the word of God.
—*Ephesians 6:17*

I pray always with all prayer and supplication in the Spirit, and I watch thereunto with all perseverance and supplication for all saints.
—*Ephesians 6:18*

And I pray for me, that utterance may be given unto me, that I may open my mouth boldly, to make known the mystery of the gospel.
—*Ephesians 6:19*

I am born of you, O God, and I overcome the world: and this is the victory that overcomes the world, even my faith.
—*1 John 5:4*

No weapon that is formed against me shall prosper; and every tongue that shall rise against me in judgment I condemn.
—*Isaiah 54:17*

If two of us shall agree on earth as touching any thing that we shall ask, it shall be done for us of our Father which is in heaven.
—*Matthew 18:19*

For though I walk in the flesh, I do not war after the flesh.
—*2 Corinthians 10:3*

For the weapons of my warfare are not carnal, but mighty through God to the pulling down of strong holds.
—*2 Corinthians 10:4*

For your word, O God, is quick, and powerful, and sharper than any twoedged sword, piercing even to the dividing asunder of soul and spirit, and of the joints and marrow, and is a discerner of the thoughts and intents of the heart.
—*Hebrews 4:12*

~ 28 ~

Believers' Triumph

Thank you, Father, that in you I am victorious and I am more than a conqueror through Jesus Christ, who loved me.

Your word declares that I am an overcomer and that I overcome by the blood of the Lamb and by the word of my testimony.

Because you are victorious, O Lord, I am also victorious, and because you reign, I also reign by one Jesus Christ and I am seated with you in heavenly places. Therefore,

I am born of you, O God, and I overcome the world: and this
is the victory that overcomes the world, even my faith.
—*1 John 5:4*

Even when I was dead in sins, you, O God, have quickened
me together with Christ, by grace I am saved.
—*Ephesians 2:5*

I am raised up together, and I sit together in
heavenly places in Christ Jesus.
—*Ephesians 2:6*

A thousand shall fall at my side, and ten thousand at
my right hand; but it shall not come nigh me.
—*Psalm 91:7*

I tread upon the lion and adder: the young lion
and the dragon I trample under feet.
—*Psalm 91:13*

I am of you, O God, and have overcome them: because
greater is he that is in me, than he that is in the world.
—*1 John 4:4*

Through you, O Lord, I push down my enemies: through
your name I thread them under that rise up against me.
—*Psalm 44:5*

I believe on you, Lord Jesus, the works that you do I do also; and
greater works than these I do; because you go unto your Father.
—*John 14:12*

You save me, O Lord my God, and gather me
from among the heathen, to give thanks unto your
holy name, and to triumph in your praise.
—*Psalm 106:47*

For you, O Lord, have made me glad through your
work: I triumph in the works of your hands.
—*Psalm 92:4*

I am more than a conqueror through you,
Christ Jesus, that loved me.
—*Romans 8:37*

For I am persuaded, that neither death, nor life, nor angels, nor
principalities, nor powers, nor things present, nor things to come,
—*Romans 8:38*

Nor height, nor depth, nor any other creature,
shall be able to separate me from your love, O
God, which is in Christ Jesus my Lord.
—*Romans 8:39*

There is therefore now no condemnation to me, I am in you,
Christ Jesus, I walk not after the flesh, but after the Spirit.
—*Romans 8:1*

I am your child, O God, then an heir; an heir of God,
and a joint-heir with Christ; if so be that I suffer with
him, that I may be also glorified together.
—*Romans 8:17*

I am made unto you, my God, a king and
priest: and I reign on the earth.
—*Revelation 5:10*

I clap my hands, I shout unto you, O God,
with the voice of triumph.
—*Psalm 47:1*

Sin does not have dominion over me: for I am
not under the law, but under grace.
—*Romans 6:14*

Lord Jesus, you give unto me the keys of the kingdom of
heaven: and whatsoever I bind on earth is bound in heaven:
and whatsoever I loose on earth is loosed in heaven.
—*Matthew 16:19*

Thanks be unto you, O God, which always
causes me to triumph in Christ.
—*2 Corinthians 2:14*

Thanks be to you, O God, which gives me the
victory through my Lord Jesus Christ.
—*1 Corinthians 15:57*

O Lord, you grant me, according to the riches of your glory, to
be strengthened with might by your Spirit in my inner man.
—*Ephesians 3:16*

Lord Jesus, you spoiled principalities and powers, you made
a shew of them openly, triumphing over them in it.
—*Colossians 2:15*

When Christ, who is my life, shall appear, then
shall I also appear with him in glory.
—*Colossians 3:4*

~ 29 ~

Anointings, Callings, and Gifts

Father God, I thank you that you have a purpose for my life, that I would be a light unto the world and show them your love. I yield to your divine plan and destiny for my life, and I surrender myself to your service.

I thank you that you have enabled me with gifts that edify and bring increase to your body. I spend time in your presence, communing with you daily, and saturating my spirit with your word.

As I walk in your love, I know you will continue to increase the anointing on my life so that you can continue to use me for your glory. Therefore, Father, I pray that

The eyes of my understanding are enlightened; that I may
know what is the hope of your calling, O God, and what
the riches of the glory of your inheritance in the saints.
—*Ephesians 1:18*

There is one body, and one Spirit, even as I am
called in one hope of your calling, O Lord.
—*Ephesians 4:4*

I am called unto liberty; I do not use liberty for an
occasion to the flesh, but by love I serve others.
—*Galatians 5:13*

I am called by your gospel, O God, to the obtaining
of the glory of my Lord Jesus Christ.
—2 Thessalonians 2:14

I come behind in no gift; I wait for the
coming of my Lord Jesus Christ.
—1 Corinthians 1:7

I have an unction from the Holy One, and I know all things.
—1 John 2:20

The anointing which I have received of you, Lord Jesus,
abides in me, and I need not that any man teaches me: but
as the same anointing teaches me of all things, and is truth,
and is no lie, and even as it has taught me, I abide in him.
—1 John 2:27

My horn you exalt, O Lord, like the horn of an
unicorn: I am anointed with fresh oil.
—Psalm 92:10

My gift makes room for me, and brings me before great men.
—Proverbs 18:16

Your gifts and calling, O God, are without repentance.
—Romans 11:29

As I have received the gift, even so I minister the same to
others, as a good steward of your manifold grace, O God.
—1 Peter 4:10

I have this treasure in my earthen vessel, that the excellency
of the power may be of you, O God, and not of me.
—2 Corinthians 4:7

You are my strength, O Lord, and you are the
saving strength of your anointed.
—Psalm 28:8

I have then gifts differing according to the grace
that is given to me, whether prophecy, I prophesy
according to the proportion of faith.
—Romans 12:6

Thank you, Father, that there are diversities
of gifts, but the same Spirit.
—1 Corinthians 12:4

Father, you are the God of all grace, you have called me unto
your eternal glory by Christ Jesus, after that I have suffered a
while, you make me perfect, stablish, strengthen, settle me.
—1 Peter 5:10

I am a chosen generation, a royal priesthood, an holy nation, a
peculiar people; that I should show forth your praises, O God,
who called me out of darkness into your marvellous light.
—1 Peter 2:9

I am a partaker of your heavenly calling, O God, I consider
the Apostle and High Priest of my profession, Christ Jesus.
—Hebrews 3:1

I covet earnestly the best gifts: yet you show
unto me, O Lord, a more excellent way.
—1 Corinthians 12:31

All things are of you, O God, you have reconciled
me to yourself by Jesus Christ, and have given
to me the ministry of reconciliation.
—2 Corinthians 5:18

I fight the good fight of faith, I lay hold on eternal
life, whereunto I am also called, and I have professed
a good profession before many witnesses.
—*1 Timothy 6:12*

I follow after charity, and I desire spiritual
gifts, but rather that I may prophesy.
—*1 Corinthians 14:1*

O God, your divine power has given unto me all things that
pertain unto life and godliness, through the knowledge of
Jesus Christ who has called me to glory and virtue.
—*2 Peter 1:3*

Forasmuch as I am zealous for spiritual gifts, I seek
that I may excel to the edifying of the church.
—*1 Corinthians 14:12*

You have stablished me in Christ, and
you have anointed me, O God.
—*2 Corinthians 1:21*

O Lord, you prepare a table before me in the presence of mine
enemies: you anoint my head with oil; my cup runs over.
—*Psalm 23:5*

O Lord, I abide in the same calling wherein I was called.
—*1 Corinthians 7:20*

I am called in you, O Lord, being a servant, I am your freeman:
likewise also I am called, being free, I am Christ's servant.
—*1 Corinthians 7:22*

Wherein I am called, therein I abide with you, O God.
—*1 Corinthians 7:24*

I walk worthy of the vocation wherewith I am called.
—Ephesians 4:1

God, you are faithful, by you I was called unto the
fellowship of your Son Jesus Christ my Lord.
—1 Corinthians 1:9

I press toward the mark for the prize of the
high calling of God in Christ Jesus.
—Philippians 3:14

I know that all things work together for my good
because I love you, O God, because I am the
called according to your purpose.
—Romans 8:28

I walk worthy of you, O God, for you have
called me unto your kingdom and glory.
—1 Thessalonians 2:12

I do not render evil for evil, or railing for railing: but
contrariwise blessing; knowing that I am thereunto
called, that I should inherit a blessing.
—1 Peter 3:9

I am your workmanship, created in Christ Jesus
unto good works, which you, O God, have before
ordained that I should walk in them.
—Ephesians 2:10

As you, O God, which have called me is holy, so
am I holy in all manner of conversation.
—1 Peter 1:15

I am your anointed, O Lord, and you save me; you hear me from
your holy heaven with the saving strength of your right hand.
—*Psalm 20:6*

And whatsoever I do in word or deed, I do all in your name,
Lord Jesus, I give thanks to God and the Father by you.
—*Colossians 3:17*

~ 30 ~

Called by God to the Gospel Ministry

Father, I thank you that you have saved me and separated me for service for such a time as this. I thank you that you have called me with a holy calling, and you have anointed me with your power and your ability to do the work of the ministry.

I study your word that I may be approved by you, a workman who needs not to be ashamed, that I would rightly divide the word of truth.

I thank you, Father, that I am your servant and I speak your word with boldness, for I am not ashamed of the gospel of Christ; it is your power, O God, unto salvation.

Thank you, Father, for calling me into the gospel ministry to lead dying humanity back to you, to help grow and mature your people in your word, O God, that they will know you and have fellowship with you. Therefore, Father,

I walk worthy of the vocation wherewith I am called.
—*Ephesians 4:1*

I walk with all lowliness and meekness, with longsuffering, forbearing others in love.
—*Ephesians 4:2*

There is one body, and one Spirit, even as I am called in one hope of your calling, O Lord.
—*Ephesians 4:4*

I walk worthy of you, O God, for you have
called me unto your kingdom and glory.
—1 Thessalonians 2:12

Thank you, O God, that you count me worthy of this
calling, and you fulfill all the good pleasure of your
goodness, and the work of faith with power.
—2 Thessalonians 1:11

I know that all things work together for my good because I love
you, O God, because I am the called according to your purpose.
—Romans 8:28

The eyes of my understanding are enlightened; that I may
know what is the hope of your calling, O God, and what
the riches of the glory of your inheritance in the saints.
—Ephesians 1:18

I am guided into all truth by the Spirit of truth
and you show me things to come.
—John 16:13

For I am not ashamed of the gospel of Christ: for it is the
power of God unto salvation to everyone that believes.
—Romans 1:16

Lord, grant unto me, your servant, that with
all boldness I speak your word.
—Acts 4:29

I am a partaker of your heavenly calling, O God, I consider
the Apostle and High Priest of my profession, Christ Jesus.
—Hebrews 3:1

I am called by your gospel, O God, to the obtaining
of the glory of my Lord Jesus Christ.
—*2 Thessalonians 2:14*

I give attendance to reading, to exhortation, to doctrine.
—*1 Timothy 4:13*

You, O God, have made me an able minister of the
new testament; not of the letter, but of the spirit: for
the letter kills, but the spirit gives me life.
—*2 Corinthians 3:6*

I press toward the mark for the prize of the
high calling of God in Christ Jesus.
—*Philippians 3:14*

I hold fast the profession of my faith without wavering;
(for you, O Lord, are faithful that promised).
—*Hebrews 10:23*

I hold forth your word of life, O God; I rejoice in the day of
Christ, that I have not run in vain, neither laboured in vain.
—*Philippians 2:16*

Your Spirit, O Lord, is upon me, because you have
anointed me to preach the gospel to the poor; you
have sent me to heal the brokenhearted, to preach
deliverance to the captives, and recovering of sight to
the blind, to set at liberty them that are bruised.
—*Luke 4:18*

You have anointed me to preach your acceptable year, O Lord.
—*Luke 4:19*

I speak as the oracles of God; I minister as of the ability
which you give, O God: that you in all things may
be glorified through Jesus Christ, to whom be praise
and dominion for ever and ever. Amen.
—*1 Peter 4:11*

It pleased you, O God, to separate me from my
mother's womb, and call me by your grace.
—*Galatians 1:15*

O Lord, you reveal your Son in me, that I
might preach him among the heathen.
—*Galatians 1:16*

I teach others to observe all things whatsoever you
have commanded me: and, lo, you are with me
always, even unto the end of the world. Amen.
—*Matthew 28:20*

I neglect not the gift that is in me, which was given me by
prophecy, with the laying on of the hands of the presbytery.
—*1 Timothy 4:14*

I meditate upon these things; I give myself wholly
to them; that my profiting may appear to all.
—*1 Timothy 4:15*

Your gifts and calling, O God, are without repentance.
—*Romans 11:29*

I am not ashamed of the testimony of my Lord, but I am partaker
of the afflictions of the gospel according to your power, O God.
—*2 Timothy 1:8*

You have saved me, and called me with an holy calling, O God, not according to my works, but according to your own purpose and grace, which was given me in Christ Jesus before the world began.
—*2 Timothy 1:9*

My gift makes room for me, and brings me before great men.
—*Proverbs 18:16*

All things are of you, O God, you have reconciled
me to yourself by Jesus Christ, and have given
to me the ministry of reconciliation.
—*2 Corinthians 5:18*

You, O God, were in Christ, reconciling me unto
yourself, not imputing my trespasses unto me; and you
have committed unto me the word of reconciliation.
—*2 Corinthians 5:19*

I am an ambassador for Christ, I am reconciled to you, O God.
—*2 Corinthians 5:20*

I give diligence to make my calling and election
sure: for if I do these things, I shall never fall.
—*2 Peter 1:10*

As you, O God, have distributed to me, as you,
O Lord, have called me, so I walk.
—*1 Corinthians 7:17*

My horn you exalt, O Lord, like the horn of an
unicorn: I am anointed with fresh oil.
—*Psalm 92:10*

O Lord, I abide in the same calling wherein I was called.
—*1 Corinthians 7:20*

I am called in you, O Lord, being a servant, I am your freeman:
likewise also I am called, being free, I am Christ's servant.
—*1 Corinthians 7:22*

I have this treasure in my earthen vessel, that the excellency
of the power may be of you, O God, and not of me.
—*2 Corinthians 4:7*

I am bought with a price; I am not the servant of men.
—*1 Corinthians 7:23*

Wherein I am called, therein I abide with you, O God.
—*1 Corinthians 7:24*

For it is you, O God, which work in me both to
will and to do of your good pleasure.
—*Philippians 2:13*

I am your sheep, Lord Jesus, I hear your voice,
and you know me, and I follow you.
—*John 10:27*

Your Spirit, O Lord God, is upon me; because you have anointed
me to preach good tidings unto the meek; you have sent me to
bind up the brokenhearted, to proclaim liberty to the captives,
and the opening of the prison to them that are bound.
—*Isaiah 61:1*

You have anointed me to proclaim your acceptable year, O Lord.
—*Isaiah 61:2*

Whatsoever I do, I do it heartily, as to
you, O Lord, and not unto men.
—*Colossians 3:23*

I am offered upon the sacrifice and service of my faith.
—*Philippians 2:17*

I am your servant, O Lord, and I do not strive; but I
am gentle unto all men, apt to teach, patient.
—*2 Timothy 2:24*

I was made a minister, according to the gift of your grace, O
God, given unto me by the effectual working of your power.
—*Ephesians 3:7*

I study to show myself approved unto you, O God, a workman
that needs not to be ashamed, rightly dividing the word of truth.
—*2 Timothy 2:15*

O Lord, you gave some, apostles; and some, prophets; and
some, evangelists; and some, pastors and teachers;
—*Ephesians 4:11*

For the perfecting of the saints, for the work of the
ministry, for the edifying of the body of Christ:
—*Ephesians 4:12*

Till we all come in the unity of the faith, and of the
knowledge of the Son of God, unto a perfect man, unto
the measure of the stature of the fulness of Christ.
—*Ephesians 4:13*

I hold the mystery of the faith in a pure conscience.
—*1 Timothy 3:9*

I speak the things which become sound doctrine.
—*Titus 2:1*

I continue in prayer, and I watch in the same with thanksgiving.
—*Colossians 4:2*

I pray also for me, that you, O God, open unto me a
door of utterance, to speak the mystery of Christ.
—*Colossians 4:3*

I make the mystery of Christ manifest, as I ought to speak.
—*Colossians 4:4*

I walk in wisdom toward them that are
without, redeeming the time.
—*Colossians 4:5*

I let my speech be always with grace, seasoned with salt,
that I may know how I ought to answer every man.
—*Colossians 4:6*

I preach Christ crucified, unto the Jews a
stumblingblock, and unto the Greeks foolishness.
—*1 Corinthians 1:23*

I am called of you, O God, and I preach Christ
the power of God, and the wisdom of God.
—*1 Corinthians 1:24*

For I see my calling, O God, how that not many wise men
after the flesh, not many mighty, not many noble, are called.
—*1 Corinthians 1:26*

I have an unction from the Holy One, and I know all things.
—*1 John 2:20*

I lay hands suddenly on no man, neither am I a
partaker of other men's sins: I keep myself pure.
—*1 Timothy 5:22*

I thank you, Christ Jesus my Lord,
you have enabled me, for that you counted me faithful,
putting me into the ministry.
—*1 Timothy 1:12*

I am your workmanship, created in Christ Jesus
unto good works, which you, O God, have before
ordained that I should walk in them.
—*Ephesians 2:10*

I am a chosen generation, a royal priesthood, an holy nation, a
peculiar people; that I should show forth your praises, O God,
who called me out of darkness into your marvellous light.
—*1 Peter 2:9*

I go therefore, and teach all nations, baptizing them in the
name of the Father, and of the Son, and of the Holy Ghost.
—*Matthew 28:19*

I exhort therefore, that, first of all, supplications, prayers,
intercessions, and giving of thanks, be made for all men.
—*1 Timothy 2:1*

I preach the word; I am instant in season, out of season; I
reprove, I rebuke, I exhort with all longsuffering and doctrine.
—*2 Timothy 4:2*

I endure hardness, as a good soldier of Jesus Christ.
—*2 Timothy 2:3*

I watch in all things, I endure afflictions, I do the work
of an evangelist, I make full proof of my ministry.
—*2 Timothy 4:5*

But the Comforter, which is the Holy Ghost, whom the Father has sent in your name, Lord Jesus, he teaches me all things, and brings all things to my remembrance, whatsoever you have said unto me.
—John 14:26

I give no offence in any thing, that the ministry be not blamed:
—2 Corinthians 6:3

I put the brethren in remembrance of these things, I am your good minister, Jesus Christ, nourished up in the words of faith and of good doctrine, whereunto I have attained.
—1 Timothy 4:6

In all things I approve myself as your minister, O God, in much patience, in afflictions, in necessities, in distresses.
—2 Corinthians 6:4

I speak your wisdom, O God, in a mystery, even the hidden wisdom, which you ordained before the world unto my glory.
—1 Corinthians 2:7

And I pray for me, that utterance may be given unto me, that I may open my mouth boldly, to make known the mystery of the gospel.
—Ephesians 6:19

I go into all the world, and I preach the gospel to every creature.
—Mark 16:15

I walk worthy of you, O Lord, unto all pleasing, I am fruitful in every good work, and I increase in your knowledge, O God.
—Colossians 1:10

For you, O God, are not unrighteous to forget my work and labor of love, which I have showed toward your name, in that I have ministered to the saints, and do minister.
—Hebrews 6:10

I am your minister, Jesus Christ, to the Gentiles, ministering
the gospel of God, that the offering up of the Gentiles might
be acceptable, being sanctified by the Holy Ghost.
—*Romans 15:16*

I have not chosen you, O Lord, but you have chosen me,
and ordained me, that I should go and bring forth fruit,
and that my fruit should remain: that whatsoever I ask of
the Father in your name, Lord Jesus, he gives it me.
—*John 15:16*

Whereof I am made a minister, according to your dispensation, O
God, which is given to me for others, to fulfil the word of God.
—*Colossians 1:25*

Lord God, the mystery which has been hid from ages and
from generations, is now made manifest to me, your saint.
—*Colossians 1:26*

To me, O God, you make known what is the riches
of the glory of this mystery among the Gentiles;
which is Christ in me, the hope of glory.
—*Colossians 1:27*

I preach you, Lord Jesus, warning every man, and
teaching every man in all wisdom; that I may present
every man perfect in you, Christ Jesus.
—*Colossians 1:28*

Whereunto I also labor, striving according to your
working, Lord Jesus, which works in me mightily.
—*Colossians 1:29*

My speech and my preaching is not with enticing words of man's wisdom, but in demonstration of the Spirit and of power.
—*1 Corinthians 2:4*

Now to you, O Lord, that is of power to stablish me according to your gospel, and the preaching of Jesus Christ, according to the revelation of the mystery, which was kept secret since the world began,
—*Romans 16:25*

But now is made manifest, and by the scriptures of the prophets, according to the commandment of the everlasting God, made known to all nations for the obedience of faith.
—*Romans 16:26*

So the last shall be first, and the first last: for many are called, but few chosen.
—*Matthew 20:16*

You have taken me from the ends of the earth, O Lord, and called me from the chief men thereof, and said unto me, "you are my servant; I have chosen you, and not cast you away."
—*Isaiah 41:9*

To God only wise, be glory through Jesus Christ for ever. Amen.
—*Romans 16:27*

Now unto him that is able to keep me from falling, and to present me faultless before the presence of his glory with exceeding joy, To the only wise God my Saviour, be glory and majesty, dominion and power, both now and ever. Amen.
—*Jude 1:24, 25*

The Lord's Prayer

My Father which is in heaven, Hallowed be your name.

Your kingdom come. Your will be done in earth, as it is in heaven.

Give me this day my daily bread.

And forgive me my debts, as I forgive my debtors.

And lead me not into temptation, but deliver me from evil: For yours is the kingdom, and the power, and the glory, forever. Amen.

—Matthew 6:9-13

Ephesians 1 Prayer

Blessed be the God and Father of my Lord Jesus Christ, who has blessed me with all spiritual blessings in heavenly places in Christ:

According as you have chosen me in you before the foundation of the world, that I should be holy and without blame before you in love:

You, Father, have predestinated me unto the adoption of children by Jesus Christ to himself, according to the good pleasure of your will,

To the praise of the glory of your grace, wherein you have made me accepted in the beloved.

In whom I have redemption through your blood, the forgiveness of sins, according to the riches of your grace;

Wherein you have abounded toward me in all wisdom and prudence;

Having made known unto me the mystery of your will, according to your good pleasure which you have purposed in yourself:

That in the dispensation of the fulness of times you might gather together in one all things in Christ, both which are in heaven, and which are on earth; even in you:

In you also I have obtained an inheritance, being predestinated according to your purpose who works all things after the counsel of your own will:

That I should be to the praise of your glory, who first trusted in Christ.

In whom I also trusted, after that I heard the word of truth, the gospel of my salvation: in whom also after that I believed, I was sealed with that holy Spirit of promise,

Which is the earnest of my inheritance until the redemption of the purchased possession, unto the praise of your glory.

I have faith in you, Lord Jesus, and love unto all the saints,

The God of my Lord Jesus Christ, the Father of glory, you give unto me the spirit of wisdom and revelation in your knowledge:

That the eyes of my understanding are enlightened; that I may know what is the hope of your calling, and what the riches of the glory of your inheritance in the saints,

And what is the exceeding greatness of your power to us-ward who believe, according to the working of your mighty power,

Which you wrought in Christ, when you raised him from the dead and set him at your own right hand in the heavenly places,

Far above all principality, and power, and might, and dominion, and every name that is named, not only in this world, but also in that which is to come:

And you have put all things under his feet and gave him to be the head over all things to the church,

Which is his body, the fulness of him that fills all in all.

Psalm 23 Prayer

You, O Lord, are my shepherd; I shall not want.

You make me to lie down in green pastures: you lead me beside the still waters.

You restore my soul: you lead me in the paths of righteousness for your name's same.

Yea, though I walk through the valley of the shadow of death, I will fear no evil: for you are with me; your rod and your staff they comfort me.

You prepare a table before me in the presence of my enemies: you anoint my head with oil; my cup runs over.

Surely goodness and mercy shall follow me all the days of my life: and I will dwell in your house, O Lord, forever.

Psalm 51 Prayer

Have mercy upon me, O God, according to your lovingkindness: according unto the multitude of your tender mercies blot out my transgressions.

Wash me thoroughly from mine iniquity, and cleanse me from my sin.

For I acknowledge my transgressions: and my sin is ever before me.

Against you, you only, have I sinned and done this evil in your sight: that you might be justified when you speak, and be clear when you judge.

Behold, I was shapen in iniquity; and in sin did my mother conceive me.

Behold, you desire truth in the inward parts: and in the hidden part, you shall make me to know wisdom.

Purge me with hyssop, and I shall be clean: wash me, and I shall be whiter than snow.

Make me to hear joy and gladness; that the bones which you have broken may rejoice.

Hide your face from my sins, and blot out all mine iniquities.

Create in me a clean heart, O God; and renew a right spirit within me.

Cast me not away from your presence; and take not your holy spirit from me.

Restore unto me the joy of your salvation; and uphold me with your free spirit.

Then will I teach transgressors your ways; and sinners shall be converted unto you.

Deliver me from bloodguiltiness, O God, thou God of my salvation: and my tongue shall sing aloud of your righteousness.

O Lord, open thou my lips; and my mouth shall show forth your praise.

For you desire not sacrifice; else would I give it: you delight not in burnt offering.

Your sacrifices, O God, are a broken spirit: a broken and a contrite heart, O God, you will not despise.

Do good in your good pleasure unto Zion: build the walls of Jerusalem.

Then shall you be pleased with the sacrifices of righteousness, with burnt offering and whole burnt offering: then shall they offer bullocks upon your altar.

Psalm 91 Prayer

I dwell in the secret place of the most High and I abide under the shadow of the Almighty.

I say of you, O Lord, you are my refuge and my fortress: my God; in you I trust.

Surely you deliver me from the snare of the fowler, and from the noisome pestilence.

You cover me with your feathers, and under your wings I trust: your truth is my shield and buckler.

I am not afraid for the terror by night; nor for the arrow that flies by day;

Nor for the pestilence that walks in darkness; nor for the destruction that wastes at noonday.

A thousand shall fall at my side, and ten thousand at my right hand; but it shall not come nigh me.

Only with my eyes shall I behold and see the reward of the wicked.

Because I have made you, O Lord, which is my refuge, even the most High, my habitation;

There shall no evil befall me, neither shall any plague come nigh my dwelling.

For you give your angels charge over me, to keep me in all my ways.

They bear me up in their hands, lest I dash my foot against a stone.

I tread upon the lion and adder: the young lion and the dragon I trample under feet.

Because I have set my love upon you, O Lord, therefore, you deliver me: you set me on high, because I know your name.

I call upon you, O Lord, and you answer me: you are with me in trouble; you deliver me, and honour me.

With long life you satisfy me, and show me your salvation.

Prayer of Salvation

Father God, I come to you in the name of Jesus Christ. I confess to you that I am a sinner and need to receive Jesus as my Savior.

I ask you to forgive me of all my sins. The Bible says that if I confess with my mouth the Lord Jesus, and believe in my heart that you have raised him from the dead, I will be saved *(Romans 10:9)*.

I believe in my heart that you raised Jesus from the dead, and I confess with my mouth that Jesus is the Lord and Savior of my life.

I believe that I am saved right now, that I have eternal life, and that I will live with you forever and ever.

Thank you, O God, for saving me! In Jesus's name I pray. Amen!

Prayer of Restoration

Heavenly Father, I come to you in the name of Jesus, realizing that I have messed up and I want to get my life right with you again.

You said in your word that if I confessed my sins, you are faithful and just to forgive me my sins and to cleanse me from all unrighteousness *(1 John 1:9)*.

Lord, I confess right now that I have sinned against you and I believe that you have forgiven me and wiped my slate clean as if I never sinned. I repent and I choose to turn away from sin and serve you with my whole heart.

I choose to saturate my spirit with your word and allow the mind that is in Christ Jesus to be in me. I hide your word in my heart that I will not sin against you, O Lord *(Psalm 119:11)*.

Thank you, O God, for restoring me! In Jesus's name I pray. Amen!

"Bless the Lord, ye his angels, that excel in strength, that do his commandments, hearkening unto the voice of his word."
—*Psalm 103:20*

Contact Information

If this book has been and is being a blessing to you, please contact me and share your story at <u>Vickie.Princebooks@gmail.com.</u>

"Know therefore that the Lord thy God, he is God, the faithful God, which keepeth covenant and mercy with them that love him and keep his commandments to a thousand generations."
—*Deuteronomy 7:9*

About the Author

Vickie Prince accepted Jesus Christ as her Lord and personal Savior and was baptized with the Holy Spirit at the age of sixteen. Vickie accepted her call to the gospel ministry in 1994 to teach God's word. She received Bible training through the Evangelical Training Association for Foundational Church Ministries. Vickie received her BS degree in Clothing, Textiles, and Related Arts from Alabama A&M University.

In 1999 God began to instruct Vickie and her husband, Elder Ollie D'Wayne Prince, to start a church in the city of Huntsville, Alabama. There she copastored as they weekly taught and preached the word of God, leading men and women to their purpose and destiny in God. After pastoring for several years, she began to sense a greater call to minister to a larger portion of the body of Christ through conferences, seminars, and meetings.

Vickie also ministers through songs with her husband and is anointed to bring the body of Christ to an intimate level of praise and worship before the presence of God Almighty. Their ministry has appeared on numerous television networks in north Alabama.

Vickie and Ollie have been married for over twenty-nine years and are the proud parents of three wonderful daughters who have been instrumental to their ministry in performing various activities for services.

Vickie is anointed to teach and preach the word of God with clarity to believers throughout the body of Christ. After writing confessional scriptures for many years, God instructed her to arrange his word into a more confessional form so that his whole body could easily commune with him by speaking his word directly to him.

It is Vickie's desire to see 1 Corinthians 1:10 become fulfilled in the body of Christ, which says, "Now I beseech you, brethren, by the name of our Lord Jesus Christ, that ye all speak the same thing, and that there be no divisions among you; but that ye be perfectly joined together in the same mind and in the same judgment."

Printed in the United States
By Bookmasters